Old Lady by the Sea

Since 1885 she has been
standing by the sea.
Standing and waiting
to fold her arms around us.
"Getting and spending
we lay waste"...
We forget our why
and our purpose.
But the old lady
steadfastly stands here in
this place to remind us.
Her nooks and crannies,
no room like any other,
memories in the hallways,
the ghost of the captain
in the attic.
With all of these, she
has created a special place
that allows us to give up
our stories to her
She will keep them safe
for our remembering.
"They also serve who
only stand and"...

Dear Diary
Food for Thought
from
Sea Crest by the Sea
by Carol Kirby

Scandalous, sexy, romantic, tender, inspiring, hilarious, and moving. This is what people say about these entries from the Sea Crest Diaries. Eight years in the writing, *Dear Diary, Food for Thought from Sea Crest by the Sea* is a collection of the best room diary entries and best breakfast and afternoon tea recipes from the Sea Crest by the Sea Bed and Breakfast Inn in beautiful Spring Lake, New Jersey.

Built in 1885, this glorious old lady by the sea just one hour from New York City, has been nurturing the weary bodies and souls of ladies and gentlemen on seaside holiday for over 100 years.

The karma of this special place has allowed her guests to reveal their stories. Now, through Carol Kirby, she gives up those stories to you. If you have ever experienced the excitement of reading someone else's diary, don't miss this one. A remarkable collection, hundreds of entries from all kinds of people, from all walks of life, famous and infamous.

The recipes are the best from the famous Sea Crest kitchen. It's the inn that *Gourmet* magazine called "a top choice," *Country Inns Bed and Breakfast* magazine selected as one of their "top inns" and *Victoria* magazine calls "a perfect ocean refuge." White chocolate cheese cake and buttermilk scones–yum!

Carol Kirby lives with her husband John and dog Daisy, and cats Sneakers and Princess in Spring Lake, New Jersey.

Published by Keepsake Enterprises, Ltd., Inc.
242 Bridgewater Drive
McDonald, Tennessee 37353

Library of Congress Catalog Number: 98-066228
ISBN: 0-9663918-0-2

Edited, typesetting, and book designed by
Dianna G. Gupton
Keepsake Enterprises, Ltd., Inc.

Cover design by
Bleichner & Bleichner
Reliance, Tennessee

Back cover photography by
George Gardner

Illustrations by
Chih-Wel Chang

Key logo used by permission
Professional Association of Innkeepers International
Santa Barbara, California

Taste testers
Ann Quesada and Luisa Jimenez

Manufactured by
Palace Press
San Francisco, California

Printed in Hong Kong

Table of Contents

Acknowledgment

The guests come first, after the staff
By putting staff first, they put guests first every day. Every day at the
Sea Crest is 50% hard work, 50% fun and 100% theater.
We have a PASSION to be the absolute BEST at what we do.
The sentiment of the Victorians was that anything worth doing was worth
doing to excess. We wholeheartedly agree, "If you are going to build a
bridge across the Mississippi, do it lengthwise."

The Sea Crest Gang of Twelve plus Daisy
Sasha Leonhardt, Innkeeper/Chef
Ann Quesada, Innkeeper/Head Housekeeper
Luisa Jiminez, Innkeeper/Housekeeper
Jason Thomson, Furniture Mover/Scholar
Charlie Plungis, Innkeeper/Handyman
Terri Thomson, Senior Innkeeper
Arthur Thomson, Innkeeper/Poet
Dannan Bernard, Innkeeper/Cruise Director
Shawn Thomson, Former bike engineer/Future owner of Rods
Jay Thomson, Former bike mechanic/Future Broadway Star
Carol Kirby, Innkeeper/Owner
John Kirby, Innkeeper/Owner
Daisy

About This Book

Muffins and Marketing "Sea Crest by the Sea" was our first cookbook. Along with our favorite recipes we included our 50 Secrets to Successful Innkeeping. Many of our guests who are aspiring innkeepers found our suggestions helpful, insightful and thought provoking. Other inngoers enjoyed the recipes and shared in the dreams.

After being at the Sea Crest for eight years, we found that our breakfast and tea repertoires had changed. We still serve many of our signature dishes, but we wanted to create a cookbook that included many of our newly developed recipes. At the same time we made the decision, we noticed that our room diaries were bursting with entries from our guests.

While having our coffee one morning, the subject of the cookbook and diaries came up. A spark flashed and *Dear Diary, Food for Thought from Sea Crest by the Sea* was born. Who said coffee blended half decaf and half regular doesn't do the job? I want to thank all of the Sea Crest staff for compiling this book; reading all of the diaries, choosing the entries, collecting all the recipes from our scraps of paper and "memory files" and most importantly, diligently testing each one. Our senior editors are Art Thomson, Sasha Leonhardt, and Dannan Bernard. Some how everyone found time for this job while being full time innkeepers as well. Many thanks.

It is with great pleasure we share our treasured recipes and some astounding, inspirational and heartfelt thoughts from our beloved guests.

So, be prepared to laugh, cry, and blush as the diaries open and reveal their secrets.

Dedication

I would like to dedicate this book to Sasha Leonhardt, our master chef and "little helper," who is responsible for preparing almost all of the delicious recipes that both the guests and we enjoy. As one of our guests said, "Sasha's breakfasts are so yummy, I wish I had an extra tummy." Thank you, Sasha, for so many wonderful breakfasts.

A very special thank you to Terri Thomson, our senior innkeeper and mom to all. She keeps our offices running, our guests smiling, and our staff coordinated. Without her, our painted lady would be far less welcoming and organized. She is the heart of the Sea Crest by the Sea and we all love her.

Introduction

The Sea Crest by the Sea's newest cookbook, *Dear Diary, Food for Thought from Sea Crest by the Sea*, has been put together as a labor of love for all of our many guest throughout the years.

Let's go to a place that's magic.
A place where we can share precious moments.
A place just for you and me.
Sea Crest by the Sea.

With you, I can be at ease and share my mind.
Friend always. Lover forever.
Come now, join me in this mystical world,
For lovers only.
Here there is no need to be afraid, not now, not ever.
Stay with me at,
Sea Crest by the Sea.

Art Thomson, Innkeeper/Poet
Dedicated to Terri, Senior Innkeeper and my lovely wife

We at Sea Crest offer this recipe and many others to all of you.

Food for Thought

1 cup of time
1 bunch of flowers
1 date for love
1 cup of romance
1 whole hug
1 pinch of spice

Mix time and flowers together with a date for love. Gradually stir in romance and a hug. A pinch of spice can be added for flavor.

These are the ingredients from which memories and love are made.

Diaries from

Key to Starters

—*The Diaries From Sleigh Ride*—
Sleigh Ride is a Winter Wonderland with a high brass featherbed
for a sleigh, a triple mirror mahogany dresser surrounded by
vintage Currier & Ives Winter Scenes, and a cozy fireplace.
It's enough to make any Santa jolly for his 'round the world ride.

9-4-90

"Just hear those sleigh
bells ringing . . ."

. . . and the chimes on
the clock jingling!

What a wonderful
place! (Makes you wish
you packed your special
Christmas underwear.)

Comfy bed, beautiful
rooms, charming people.

Great coffee! (Request
the popovers.)

It's so nice to stay
somewhere that's as nice
as -- or nicer -- than
your own bedroom.

Rosemary & Frank

*A great source for unusual soups is
"The Enchanted Broccoli Forest"*

Almond Soup

3-4 servings

*1¼ cups chopped, blanched (skinless) almonds
2 tablespoons butter
½ cup chopped onion
1 large clove garlic, crushed
½ teaspoon freshly minced ginger
½ teaspoon salt
1¾ cups water or stock
1½ cups fresh squeezed orange juice
1-2 tablespoons dry sherry
½ teaspoon fresh orange rind
Black pepper to taste
Cayenne pepper to taste*

*Serve with:
Slivered toasted almonds
Finely minced chives
Thin rounds of fresh orange*

In a heavy skillet, cook the almonds in butter with onion, garlic, ginger and salt over a low flame. Stir until the almonds are toasty and the onions are soft, 8 to 10 minutes. Remove from heat.

Using a blender or food processor fitted with a steel blade, puree the sautéed mixture in combined water (or stock) and orange juice. Add sherry to taste. Make sure the puree is very smooth. Transfer to a kettle or saucepan.

Stir in the orange rind and the black and cayenne pepper. Heat the soup gently (just heat-don't cook it). Serve soup as soon as it is hot and garnish each serving with assorted delightful toppings.

11

APRIL 24, 1993

9-30-93

With a single smile, he became
my world!

Jiley

Chilled Cantaloupe-Peach Soup

Delicious and light.
Perfect as a compliment to a rich meal or as a desert on a hot day.

Preparation time: 30 minutes
Chill: 3 hours minimum
Yield: 12 servings

6 medium sized ripe peaches
¼ cup B & B or Grand Marnier
6 tablespoons fresh lemon juice (approximately the equivalent of
juice from one large, juicy lemon)
¼ teaspoon cinnamon or more to taste
Dash of nutmeg
Mace to taste
1 medium-size (5-inch diameter) ripe cantaloupe
1 cup fresh orange juice
Blueberries for garnish

Peel, pit and slice the peaches. Place peaches in a heavy saucepan with Grand Marnier, lemon juice, cinnamon, nutmeg, and mace. Heat to a boil; lower to simmer, cover, and let stew for 10 minutes. Cool to room temperature.

Using a blender or food processor, puree the peach mixture with all its liquid. Return the puree to a serving bowl.

Chop approximately three-fourths of the cantaloupe (minus skin and seed, of course) and puree in the orange juice until smooth; add to the peach puree. Mince the remaining melon and add pieces. Cover and chill. Serve very cold. Garnish with blueberries.

Dear Carol + John,   10/24/93

    Your hospitality +
warmth are unmatched +
have made this weekend
truly memorable.

    The food was delectable
and the room was extremely
romantic. (sorry about all the
noise!)

    Great way to spend our
16 month anniversary.

    We'll Be Back!
        Bonnie + Dave

4/17; 18; 19; 20   April 20, 1994

Dear Carol and John,
    We're certainly glad to be back
again! Our spring ~~your~~ break—
what a great get away. The
weather 84° yesterday was just
superb.
    Once again many thanks to you
both and to your staff as well
who make us feel most welcome.
Breakfast is just superb — we
thoroughly enjoy it.
    Looking forward to seeing you
again in the summer.

                    Fondly,
                    Helen and Al
                    May 11, 1994
Dear Kirby's,   We are slightly care-
less and most definetly ear less. In
spite of all this we're having a great
Time!
                    Ellie and Bill

Honeymoon   1/26/95
        Thank's so much John
& Carol for a lovely time.
This is a new beginning
for Bob & I, we will cherish
this place in our hearts.
        The food was outragouss
& wonderful to the palet.
We were very content &
satisfied with all the
gracious atmosphere.

                    Yours Truly,
                    Sally & Bob

P.S. God Bless you, and
may the Lord shine his face
upon you. ⊂≻ Let us pray
for him to perfect our spelling &
grammar.

16

Watermelon Gazpacho

Sweet, spicy and very refreshing
We use our juicer for the watermelon juice, that is the base of this soup.
If you do not have one, a blender or food processor will work very well and
your soup will be a little thicker. We always use seedless watermelons.
They cost a little more, but they save you a lot of work.

Yield: 6 cups

$2\frac{1}{2}$ *cups ($\frac{1}{2}$ melon) watermelon juice*
2 tomatoes
1 cucumber
3 green onions
1-3 jalepeños

Juice or puree the watermelon. Dice tomatoes, cucumber, onions and jalepeños. Combine and chill overnight.

Creamy Bulgar with Pears

Serves 4

2 cups skim milk
$\frac{1}{2}$ cup water
1 cup bulgar (cracked wheat)
$\frac{1}{4}$ teaspoon salt
2 ripe pears, diced
$\frac{1}{2}$ cup chopped walnuts
$\frac{1}{3}$ cup maple syrup

Bring milk, water, and salt to a boil in large saucepan. Stir in bulgar. Reduce heat and simmer, uncovered, for 15 minutes. Remove from heat and cover; let stand. Stir in pears, walnuts, and maple syrup. Serve warm.

May .1, 1995   Life is very short
somtimes you win somtimes you lose,
IF I can not find true Happyness in
this life I must beleeve I was
created For another life. Are you
Happy this day or our you just being
what you Know to be or trying to be
somthing you think you should be.
life is short Find whats true or
Who's true. As For the room I
Have nothing to say.

Love
LiFe

Feb 26, 1997

This inn is a bit different from what we are normally used to. It is very romantic... almost magical... as we entered our sleigh Ride kingdom, my love, reverted to his boyish ways. First he took off my dress and shoes and tenderly massaged my toes — very neat. Next, my bra and panties were flung to the floor — not so neat. Making love in this enchanted room with the love of my life was... well, make your own fantasy. After breakfast tomorrow our fantasy ends and its back to the real world, well at least we will have the memories to take with us.

Sarah & Donald
NYC.

It has been a wonderful 3 day respite from exams, grade books, meetings, etc. Looking forward to a third visit!

Leanne
Holland Patent, NY

P.S. Baxter + Spanky really liked jumping up · down on the feather bed !!

DEAR JOHN AND CAROL,

THE MOMENT MY EYES LAID UPON THIS WINTER WONDERLAND MY DARLING CARMELINA AND I HAD VISIONS OF SUGAR PLUM FAIRIES AND SUNANRIAHA IN OUR HEADS. IT WAS THE MOST INCREDIBLE EXPERIENCE IN OUR OTHERWISE DULL LIVES. YOU SEE, WE BOTH WORK SEVEN DAYS A WEEK AND NEEDED TO "SPARK UP" OUR RELATIONSHIP. THANKS SO MUCH FOR THE WARMTH AND GENEROSITY THAT YOU BOTH EXHIBITED.

PEACE AND

LOVE,

PEE WEE AND

DON THE DRILL

Mediterranean Lemon Soup

This is a wonderful soup to serve with Greek Frittata
(recipe on page 49)
Good hot or cold.

2 tablespoons butter
1 cup finely minced onion
1 teaspoon salt
A few grindings of fresh, black pepper
1 teaspoon dried, crushed mint
1 cup cooked brown rice or barley
½ cup freshly squeezed lemon juice
2 cups stock or water

Toppings:
Freshly minced parsley
Freshly minced chives
Yogurt, sour cream or heavy cream
Grated hard cooked eggs

In a soup size saucepan, sauté the onion in butter with salt and pepper until the onion is soft and translucent.

Add the rice or barley. Add the water (or stock), lemon juice, and mint. Heat, covered, over a low flame until it boils gently.

November 18, 1997

Although we planned this vacation (even if it was for one night) very far in advance, I should not have hoped that my husband would keep his promise to not let anything come between us and our romantic excursion. But, here I am, at the Sea Crest and all _alone_! Nothing like a bunch of happy couples around to make one feel even more lonely. I suppose I should not complain so much, I was the one who married a doctor. But sometimes I have to wonder what is more important, his wife or his work! I was hoping this overnight getaway would be a chance for us to get to know each other better, "fall in love again" but instead I am almost ready to leave him for good _this time_, Sure, that's probably just the wine talking, Thank you Sea Crest for making my stay tolerable, and thank you for this diary, at least I had "someone" to talk to on my lonely vacation.

Carmen

P.S.

Next day - well maybe it was not the wine talking last night. It is amazing how a walk on the beach can clear one's head. While down there I met Paul, I am leaving now to have lunch with him! Perhaps someday I will return to Sea Crest with someone who will keep his promise!!

22

Hot Fruit Compote

The aroma of this cooking will make early risers out of everyone.
This is a great alternative to fresh fruit in the winter months.
It is also good on top of Whiskey Oats or even pancakes.

Serves 8

1 cup chopped mixed dried fruit
1 fresh apple, chopped
1 ripe pear, chopped
½ cup grapes, sliced in half
½ cup water
½ cup orange juice
¼ cup Grand Marnier
½ teaspoon cloves
½ teaspoon cinnamon
½ teaspoon ground mace
½ teaspoon ginger

Combine all ingredients in a saucepan. Cover and simmer for 30 minutes or until the liquid is absorbed.

Pear Melon Soup

¼ cup lemon juice
6 pears, peeled and cored
1 honeydew melon
1 teaspoon ginger
1 cup white wine
Raspberries for garnish

Put all lemon juice, pears, honeydew melon, ginger, and white wine in food processor and blend until smooth. Serve chilled. Garnish with fresh raspberries.

Diaries from

Key to Sweet Breakfasts

—The Diaries from Victorian Rosebud—
Before the change, Victorian Rosebud was Flamingo Grove.
Then, in 1995 we were overwhelmed by a brass canopy bed.
With so much Lilliputian Luxury the room had to become
the Victorian Rosebud. Small, but luxurious,
it always seems to attract our most romantic couples.

There's a charming place
        by the Jersey shore
Where flamingoes stroll
        'round the second floor
And a velveteen rabbit
        may tap at your door
    Sea Crest - by the sea

Fear not! - if you're joggers,
        or swimmers or sitters
The coffee they blend
        will not give you the jitter
And the place has the friendliest
        four-legged critters
    Sea Crest - by the sea

The transport is two-wheeled,
        or four-wheeled, or three
('tho the three-wheeled affair
        is used mainly by me -
but I'll share in the interest
        of sweet harmony)
    Sea Crest - by the sea

Daisy Mae and George Washington
　　　wait for your call
As do Teddy and Bogey
　　　and Lauren Bacall
Papillons fill the air
　　　'round the Mardi Gras bal
Sea Crest - by the sea.

They've a stumpfiddle and a
　　　piano to play
The excitement of John's "famous"
　　　bread of the day
A croquet tournement
　　　with an "e", not an "a"
Sea Crest - by the sea

Carol's breakfast buffet
　　　delights body and soul
Then let South End Pavilion laps
　　　be your next goal
3, you won't need to drive
　　　out of here, you'll just woe
Sea Crest - by the sea.

It's quite easy to reach
        on the New Jersey line
When you're ~~bound~~ ed for Spring Lake
        the whole journey seems fine
And tonight, after Lotto,
        this all could be <u>MINE</u>
Sea Crest - by the sea

                        Claire-Anne
                        September 3, 1990
P.S. But if you think that
I'm going to stay up nights
baking breads for people in the
greater tri-state area, you've
been "by the sea" too long.

After extensive testing in the Sea Crest kitchen, thank you taste testers,
we have all agreed the perfect pancake comes from a box.
They come out perfect every time, are so easy, and can take anything you want to
combine with them. These are some of our favorite pancake flavors.
They are all for two cups of mix and can be multiplied.

Lemon Ricotta Pancakes

½ cup lemon juice
½ cup ricotta cheese
1 teaspoon lemon peel

Substitute lemon juice for ½ cup water or milk. Add ricotta cheese and lemon peel to pancake batter. Cook according to package directions

Apple Cinnamon Pancakes

1 cup grated apple
1 teaspoon cinnamon
1 teaspoon vanilla

Add apple, cinnamon, and vanilla to pancake batter. Cook according to package directions.

Banana Rum Pancakes

¼ cup rum or 1 teaspoon rum extract
2 cups mashed bananas
½ teaspoon nutmeg

Substitute rum for ¼ cup water or milk, or just add rum extract. Add bananas and nutmeg to pancake batter. Cook according to package directions.

Lemon Blueberry Pancakes

½ cup lemon juice
1 cup blueberries

Substitute lemon juice for ½ cup water or milk. Add blueberries to batter. Cook according to package directions.

July 22, 23, 24 & 25 –

Came in feeling blue
& left feeling "tickled
pink". I can now rest
easy knowing where the
sea gulls sleep . . .

E & S

August 10, 1994

Once a flamingo
always a
Flamingo
Dorothy

Coconut Custard French Toast

*If you choose, this toast can be prepared and refrigerated
the night before serving.
We use bread machine bread, potato is our favorite. If you do not have a
bread machine, use bakery style or thick sliced.
Our french toast recipes are not recommended for "Wonder Bread."*

Serves 12

1 loaf bread
15 eggs
1 cup half-and-half
1 cup heavy cream
½ cup frozen pina colada mix
2 teaspoons vanilla
¼ cup rum
7 ounces sweet, shredded coconut
1 stick butter

Spray a 9 x 13-inch pan with non-stick cooking spray. Trim the crust off the bread and slice in half. Lay in pan, partially standing up.

Combine eggs, half-and-half, heavy cream, pina colada mix, vanilla, and rum. Use an electric mixer and whip well. Sprinkle coconut between slices, reserving some for the top. Pour the liquid mixture over the bread. Sprinkle the remaining coconut on top. Slice the butter into tablespoons and place over top of bread.

Refrigerate for 45 minutes. Bake, covered, at 350 degrees for 1 hour. Uncover and bake for an additional 30 minutes. Serve with maple syrup.

10/10/94

John & Carol,

Thanks for another wonderful Columbus Day Weekend. Both the weather and company were perfect. We discovered how romantic Flamingos can be! Thanks for also, making our 3rd anniversary a memorable one.

Jane & Marc

JAN 4, 1995   Happy New Year!!

Magician Ben Duke & His Lovely assistant Miss Rogers Think this place is great!! First B+B for Ben, He'll do it again!!

32

Rum Raisin French Toast

For a hearty winter breakfast or brunch, serve this toast with our
Rosemary Roasted Potatoes and Sausage.
We use homemade raisin bread from our bread machine.

Serves 12

1½ loaves raisin bread
15 eggs
1 cup half-and-half
1 cup whole milk
¼ cup dark rum
1 teaspoon vanilla
2 teaspoons cinnamon
1 cup raisins
1 stick of butter

Spray a 9 x 13-inch pan with non-stick cooking spray. Trim crusts off bread and slice in half. Lay into pan, partially standing up.

Combine eggs, half-and-half, milk, rum, vanilla, and cinnamon. Use an electric mixer and whip well. Sprinkle raisins between slices, reserving some for the top.

Pour liquid mixture over bread. Sprinkle with remaining raisins. Slice butter in tablespoons and place over top of bread. Refrigerate for 45 minutes or overnight.

Bake, covered, at 350 degrees for 1 hour. Uncover and continue to bake for an additional 30 minutes. Serve with maple syrup.

9-21-97

What a fantastic end to summer!
Everything was wonderful, the
Hosts, the Food, the Place!
P.S. Art, we enjoyed our talk on
Saturday night about these writings.
By the way the bed in the Victorian Rose
does squeak & bang the wall (hint,
check when newly weds stay!).

Larry & Debbie

Carl + Mary

Nov 10, 1997

Wow it's gotten cold outside, it a good thing I
have this nice warm body next to me to keep
me toasty. I am shocked that we both fit into
this room at the same time, but the bed seems
to have plenty of space, unlike the bathroom. At
least it is a great way to get closer to the one you love.
Maybe the living room isn't that small after all, it
was just the right size to make this a very romantic
vacation

Apple Sausage Crêpes a la B & B

This crêpe recipe is from Manor House in Cape May, N.J.

Makes 6 - 8 servings

Crêpes:
¾ cup all-purpose flour
½ teaspoon salt
1¼ cups milk
1 egg
1 egg yolk
1 tablespoon melted butter

Filling:
6 Granny Smith apples, peeled and cubed
¼ cup butter
2 tablespoons rosemary
¼ cup B & B liqueur
Sugar to taste
Breakfast sausage links, fully cooked
Sliced apples for garnish
Fresh rosemary for garnish

For crêpes:
Blend flour, salt, milk, egg, egg yolk, and butter until smooth. Using a greased crêpe pan or skillet, make crêpes. Set aside on waxed paper.

For filling:
Sauté apples in butter, rosemary, liqueur, and sugar, until soft.

Prepare crêpes:
Fill each crêpe with a breakfast sausage link and apple mixture. Fold sides of crêpe over and place in a greased oven proof pan. Repeat until all crêpes are filled. Bake at 325 degrees until golden brown. Garnish with apple slices and fresh rosemary. Maple syrup is optional.

8/26 SAT SUN 8/27 MON 8/28
3 SUPER DAYS LUCKY TO
SECURE A RESERVATION,
AT LAST MINUTE FOR A
NIFTY WK END, IN THE
SMALL TINY FLAMINGO
BED ROOM REMINDS ONE
A SMALL FRENCH HOTEL
WITH MINIMUM SPACE
AND A NEED FOR SLIM FIGURES.
THE "NON-CALORIC" BREAKFASTS
WERE A TREAT, BUT THE
DECAFFINATED TEA SAVED
THE DAY FOR A HEALTH
FADIST.
WHISPERS WAS GREAT.
THE OLD MILL A BIG
DISAPPOINTMENT.
OUR CONCIERGE (JOHN)
WAS SPLENDID.
OUR BEHAVIOR SUCH
THAT WE MAY NOT
BE ASKED BACK.

Diaries from

Victorian Rose

Key to Savory Breakfasts

—The Diaries from Victorian Rose—
Our favorite Romantic Victorian.
The most weddings, the most anniversaries, the most birthdays,
a most typical Victorian this Victorian Rose.
If anything is worth doing, it is worth doing to excess.
Her diaries reflect her nature.

January 5, 1991

Sergio and I got married last night and drove up this morning to this lovely home. Due to deadlines our honeymoon is a bit short, but we will surely return in the summer time to enjoy the beach and pleasantries of summer time. A lovely town — a lovely home.

Sergio & Nancy

For a few minutes we will be cozying up by the fire — and sparks are sure to fly!

PS: They did!

Featherbed Eggs

Our signature entree–this dish can also be prepared the night before, only to be popped into the oven an hour before breakfast. We've listed our favorite variations, but be sure to experiment with your own creations.

14 eggs
1½ cups half-and-half
Salt, pepper, and herbs of your choice to taste
1½ cups milk
Approximately 8 cups cubed or shredded bread, any heavy crusts removed

Butter a 9 x 11-inch baking dish. In a large bowl, beat eggs until frothy. Add milk and half-and-half; beat again until well blended. Place bread cubes into prepared dish, they should fill the dish approximately three-fourths full. Slowly pour egg mixture over bread. Season to taste. Cover and refrigerate for 45 minutes. Bake for approximately 1 to 1½ hours at 350 degrees until lightly browned and puffed like a featherbed!

This is the basic recipe. Here are some of our favorite variations, accomplished by simply tucking the added ingredients into the mixture after it is assembled in the pan.

Sautéed sliced mushrooms, fresh rosemary, thyme, and sage.

Shredded cheddar, mozzarella, Swiss cheese or any combination of cheeses.

Dollops of salsa and sour cream, with fresh cilantro and shredded Monterey Jack cheese (known in our kitchen as "Terri's Mexican Featherbeds").

Parboiled broccoli flowerets and shredded Swiss cheese.

Diced ham, bacon or sausage with any shredded cheese.

Slivered sun-dried tomatoes, fresh basil, and shredded mozzarella.

2/29/92

It has been over a year since our last vacation together. This weekend away has been very romantic and relaxing.

The room is beautiful and the ocean view magnificent!

Jack is asleep by my side as the sun sets. The fire feeds in the fireplace bathes the room in a warm glow & gently gurgles and sighs. I indulge in the romance of Victoria magazine.

I am happy.

5/3/92

When life becomes too much to bear I close my eyes and dream of Sea Crest!

Denise

Creamy Scrambled Eggs

We first learned of this method for scrambled eggs from
Linda and Mark at the Hollycroft Inn in South Belmar, N.J.

Serves 8

2 tablespoons butter
12 eggs
1 cup milk or half-and half or heavy cream
Herbs to taste
Salt and pepper to taste
2 tablespoons flour
2 tablespoons butter
½ cup sour cream

Melt the butter in a large non-stick pan. With an electric mixer, combine the eggs, milk, and seasonings. Make a roux with the flour, butter, and sour cream, mixing together until smooth. Set aside.

Pour eggs in the heated pan, stirring until three-fourths cooked. Add the roux mixture and continue cooking until roux is melted and eggs are fully cooked. Serve immediately.

May 15, 16, 17, 1992

We came down to Spring Lake for my sister's wedding and loved staying at the SeaCrest in Victorian Rose — although we felt a tad guilty that we — not the newlyweds — spent the most romantic weekend of all!

We are already working on our next excuse to come back!

Cathy & Scott

Nov. 14, 1992.   Alissa and Jeanne

I enjoyed Bed and Breakfast. This is my first time in new Jersy I like it. Thanks you for your service. Alissas and Jeanne

Bellevue, Washington

42

Dutch Onion Pie

An onion lover's delight. Especially good with Vidalia onions.

Serves 6 to 8

2 tablespoons butter or margarine
3 cups thinly sliced onions
1 pound cottage cheese
½ cup heavy cream
Salt and pepper to taste
Dash of cayenne
1 9-inch pie shell, baked

Fry onions in butter until soft. Moisten cheese with cream and pour into baked pie shell. Season lightly with salt and pepper. Cover with onions. Add more salt and pepper and the cayenne. Bake in pre-heated 400 degree oven for 15 minutes. Cut into wedges and serve.

The Lord has truly blessed us
with a "beautiful" world! The
breathtaking view of the ocean
from this room is wonderful.
We have filled our hearts with
many "special" memories from
our stay here.
                    Wendy & David
                    Mount Joy, PA

PS We ~~█████~~ till our
noses bled!

February 13, 1993.
  Our 1st wedding
anniversary and second
visit to Sea Crest by
the Sea. God has
truly blessed us!
Thank you John & Carol
for the wonderful
stay & breakfast. too!
                    Richie & BJ
                    Stewartsville, NJ.

P.S. She ~~█████~~ my
~~████~~ till my nose bled!

44

VICTORIAN ROSE

6-27-93

All over the wall, in tiny rows
Your green + pink grows and grow

At night while ~~I am~~ sleeping
Right under my nose
Sweet fragrance I smell
Which everyone knows
Can only be made
by a! Victorian Rose!

JAMES

April 21, 1994
This is a delightful place.
Since warm & friendly hospitality
makes me want to return for more.
Cheers

PS- This is special today because I brought my
penpal, since 8th grade, whom I never met till now, from Japan.

June 13 & 14 1994

Well, we're back for our 2ND.
anniversary - we only stayed for
one night, but that's all we
needed! There's just something
about this room that brings out
the romantic in us! We even
recreated our first dance as
husband and wife by moonlight!
Something that never would have
happened without the help of
the mood and atmosphere of
the Victorian Rose. We can't wait
for next year & more moonlight
dances.

Our Love
Susie & Nuris

TOMS RIVER, NEW JERSEY

46

Basic Frittata

You need a large skillet that is oven proof to cook eggs on top of the stove, then finish them in the oven.
We use copper pans, but anything without plastic will work well.

Serves 12

20 eggs
¾ cup half-and-half
¾ cup whole milk
4 teaspoons butter

Preheat oven to 375 degrees.

Mix with an electric mixer, eggs, milk, and half-and-half. Add seasonings of your choice.

Melt butter in the pan on medium heat. Scramble the egg mixture until three-fourths cooked. Turn off the heat. Add toppings and place in the oven for 20-30 minutes or until the eggs are cooked and rising.

You can use this basic frittata recipe and add whatever toppings you like. Greek Frittatas, Apple Cheddar Frittatas (see recipes on page 49), Mexican Frittatas, Country Frittatas (see recipes on pages 55), Pasta Primavera Frittatas, Smoked Salmon/Asparagus Cream Cheese Frittatas (see recipes on page 57), and Sesame Frittata (see recipe on page 59) are some of our favorites.

7/17/94

Well, we've had another wonderful weekend and the shared experience with our friends Barbara & Leon. This place seems to do the trick. It manages to calm the most hyper person. Hope we can return soon to enjoy the peacefulness.

Diane & Joel
Suffern NY.

7/27/94

What a great choice my wife made. I know she was here in spirit with me, Susan and Steve. John and Carol are the best host.

If and when I remarry I will bring my new wife back. I may even come again even if I don't. Mary Lee make me promise to come if she couldn't. Thank you John and Carol.

Mark
Hastings, Pa.

48

Greek Frittata

Seasonings for eggs:
Garlic
Basil
Salt and pepper

Topping:
1 cup thawed and drained frozen spinach
1 cup diced tomato or ½ cup sun-dried tomatoes
½ cup diced roasted or fresh red pepper
1 cup shredded mozzarella cheese
1 cup sliced black olives
4 ounces crumbled feta cheese

Prepare basic frittata (recipe on page 47). Season eggs and top with toppings. Go easy on the salt, the feta cheese is very salty.

Apple Cheddar Frittata

Seasonings for eggs:
Garlic
Rosemary
Thyme
Parsley
Salt and pepper

Topping:
2 large apples, sliced (we like Fuji apples)
1 teaspoons lemon juice to keep the apples from browning
1½ cups cheddar cheese, shredded
Bacon, crumbled (optional)

Prepare basic frittata (recipe on page 47). Season eggs. Slice the apples ¼-inch thick and sprinkle them with lemon juice. Once the eggs are ready, add the cheddar cheese and then apples in a circular design, like a tart. Sprinkle with crumbled bacon, if desired.

November 3, 1994

We arrived as two high school sweethearts seperated for 28 years and by three thousand miles. In the peace and solitude of this Victorian Rose cocoon we unraveled the mystery of our coming apart a lifetime ago, reveled in each memory unearthed, drowned in a passion renewed and was reborn, again to find ourselves back at the begining. The magic of finding each other again and in the same mind and need is not the fare of ordinary life. It is of the fabric the gods use to fashion the garments of legend. This is what life and love are meant to be. We arrived as two people, but only one life, one soul, one body left.

Pennie & Andre
(ANDRE)

Beth & Jerry

February 2, 1995

The trials and tribulations of a couple involved in a long distance relationship.

Pittsburg, & S. N.J

What to do?

When the Pittsburg dweller has business in Philadelphia, only 3 hours from the L.S Dweller, why not meet 1/2 way - Each to drive 1 1/2 hours and meet in a B&B Called Sea Crest by the Sea -

Ah, reunions are such Bliss!! Heavenly, romantic, sensual,,,, A place we will return to again someday soon. Room has great energy - Lots of LOVE!! AHHHHHH.

51

Feb. 20, 1995

In the words of
    John Denver

".... Didn't get much
sleep ...   but we
had a lot of fun
on 'John + Carol's'
featherbed."

                Madonna
                    +
                    ?

                            Feb. 24, 1995

    There are many Ave's of Life,
I came here this weekend to figure
them out. I left here and
decided the most important of
all, I decided to try to get
back on the road.

                    Lynn C.

52

December 29th 1996

Yes, yes yes, SeaCrest is lovely but you should let daisy out during breakfast. That would bring the homely experience full circle by allowing us to feed tbk scraps to her the way we would at home.

Chris Holt — Thanks so much for the great accomodation & hospitality. Debbie.

53

March 31, 1996

When we will come back to our
country we will ever have a very
good remembers of this lovely
weekend at Sea Creast
   Thanks for all and
   congratulations for your
   great Inn.

Soon we will come back!

   Steffen   (GERMANY)

and Laura   (MEXICO)

P.s. Allen nach uns wüschen wir eine
super Zeit hier.
Abendessen im Old Mill - einfach Spitze.

   Viel Spaß + Tschüß   Steff

54

Mexican Frittata

Seasonings for eggs:
Garlic
Cilantro
Salt and pepper

Toppings:
Salsa (use our recipe on page 165 or your favorite jar salsa)
Cheddar cheese
Monterey Jack cheese

Prepare basic frittata (see recipe on page 47). Season eggs and top with toppings.

Country Frittata

Seasoning for eggs:
Basil
Garlic
Thyme
Salt and pepper

Toppings:
4 tablespoons butter
1 onion
1 green pepper
2 large baked potatoes, diced
½ cup mushrooms
1 cup cheddar cheese, shredded

Prepare basic frittata (see recipe on page 47). Season eggs. Sauté onions and peppers in butter. Combine with potatoes, mushrooms, and cheese and top eggs.

February 2, 1997

This weekend provided the first intimate respite for my husband and I since the death of our daughter Hannah. The walks by the ocean gave me the breaths of life; having my husband by my side gave me hope and love. I love him more than our five years of marriage altogether could imaginably provide.

Yes, the Bed & Breakfast was beautiful. Yes, our room was wonderful as well as the breakfast, Daisy and tea.
Most memorable though, is my heart's first feeling of love again.
Life does go on; and oh so much nicer with a lover, friend, husband

Katrina and Sean

Pasta Primavera Frittata

Seasoning for eggs:
Garlic
Basil
Parsley
Salt and pepper

Toppings:
The toppings can be made the day before.
Just heat the Alfredo sauce and combine with toppings.
½ cup sliced mushrooms
2-4 tablespoons butter
1 diced onion
1 diced red pepper
1 sliced zucchini
1½ pounds pasta, cooked
Alfredo Sauce (see recipe on page 161)

Prepare basic frittata (see recipe on page 47). Season eggs. Sauté mushrooms, peppers, and zucchini in butter. Combine with pasta and Alfredo sauce and top eggs.

Smoked Salmon/Asparagus Cream Cheese Frittata

Seasonings for eggs:
Salt
Dill
Lemon pepper

Toppings:
1 cup smoked salmon, cut in bite-size pieces
1 pound asparagus, cleaned, peeled and steamed
½ cup cream cheese

Prepare basic frittata (see recipe on page 47). Season eggs and top with salmon and asparagus. Cut cream cheese in teaspoons and place on top.

figuratively
& literally

Sesame Frittata

This dish is a favorite of our international choices for the breakfast table.
Serve with Curried Ham Potatoes or Mushroom Brie Strudel.

30 eggs
1 quart half-and-half
1½ tablespoons sesame seed oil
¼ cup soy sauce
Salt and pepper
4 tablespoons butter

Topping:
3 ounces cream cheese, softened and spreadable
1 cup chopped watercress
2 tablespoons sesame seeds, toasted

Prepare eggs as for basic frittata (see recipe on page 47) and put in oven to bake at 400 degrees. When eggs are puffing up, spread softened cream cheese on top and put back in oven to melt.

Toast sesame seeds in a non-stick frying pan over medium-high heat, stirring until golden brown. Before serving, sprinkle on sesame seeds and watercress.

1997

May 13th & 14th

John + Carol,

We came here for the first time to escape from the everyday life. The past couple of years have been tough! I had a fatal stroke, and in the past month my best Fried lost her life to cancer. She was only 28, and I had my stroke at age 31. Tough life so far. We promised ourselves when it was over with my girlfriend we would get away for a couple of Days! Well your pamlet came at the right time,...

Diane + Craig

Trenton, NJ

July 28-30, 1997

Becky + Andy's Recipe for a
Romantic Getaway
2 people who love each other
1 romantic room (like Victorian Rose
@ Seacrest by the Sea!)

And the following optional ingredients:
1 beautiful, dramatic thunderstorm at
    night to watch from the porch
2 sunny days at the beach
1 swim in the refreshingly cool Atlantic
1 bike ride on old-fashioned 3 speeds
2 wonderful dinners out, w/reservations
    made by staff (such luxury!)
    Strolls on the boardwalk (to taste) or
        on the beach at sunset (or after)
LOTS of snuggling in the room
1 classic movie
2 luxuriously soft + silky cotton sheets
LOTS of pillows
1 ~~_____~~ Victorian f-ing couch
2 yummy breakfasts
LOTS of giggles
LOTS of kisses
LOTS of fun

Thank you Seacrest by the Sea for this delicious concoction! We are here to celebrate our 7th anniversary, which was actually July 14th, but when we checked out the Seacrest web page (nicely done, by the way!) we decided Victorian Rose was worth waiting for. Suffice it to say we were not disappointed!

We have a challenging year ahead of us, as Andy is just finishing his Ph.D in Philosophy and I already have a Ph.D in English (practical, I know, I know) and now we need to find 2 tenure-track jobs close together. It's scary, exciting, + stressful all at once... but a mini- ~~vacation~~ like this gives us the strength + courage we need to keep our chins up and keep dreaming of what tomorrow may bring.

Thanks again for an inspirational vacation.

Sincerely,

Becky
Westminster, MD

This room exudes romance and love. Who knew that the Victorians —or we ~~~~ - could have it so good?

Andy
7-30-97

Diaries from

Key to Potatoes

—The Diaries of G. Washington—
The French Art Nouveau featherbed gives it away.
George did a lot more than chop down cherry trees
and lead the nation. Some of the diary entries
claim that they saw him smile.

Oct. 14, 1990
Thanks for a wonderful time. We think George W. even cracked a smile above the bed. We will never think of our first president in the same way again.
Oh - we gotta go - the British are coming!!

Mary Beth & Bob

November 12, 1990
Good rest. Beautiful day! Having served the patriot George, we'll be on our way.
Jeff + Denise

April 14, 1991
We had a great time here and made lots of new memories. "old George had fun, too". We'll be back for more -
Susan + Greg

The beds were very comfortable! The breakfast was absolutely amazing. Being English though, we felt a bit weird sleeping under George Washington.

Victoria and Judy

May 4, 1992

Everything was sensational from the furnishings, on down to the linens! The American flag has taken on an entirely new meaning for the both of us! Thank you

Dave and Brenda

May 15-17, 1992

We truly enjoyed "entertaining" George and Martha during our visit to your lovely home.

Our 13th anniversary is full of wonderful memories. Your warmth and hospitality only added to our getaway weekend! This was our first experience with a B&B and I think we got spoiled." We'll be back!

Rick & Sammy

P.S. If only George could talk.. You know he could never tell a lie!!!

Everybody loves potatoes—baked, roasted, fried or whipped. Since our old painted lady "The Sea Crest" is in Spring Lake, also known as the Irish Riviera, we could not let a day go by without potatoes as part of our breakfast. Usually served as a side dish at breakfast, our potato recipes are fun, elegant, easy to prepare and can be part of dinner as well.

Seasoned Potato Wedges

Good anytime—try them as an hors d'oeuvre

Serves 6

⅓ cup flour
⅓ cup Parmesan cheese
1 teaspoon paprika
3 potatoes, each cut into 8 wedges
Butter
Sour cream and chives

Preheat oven to 400 degrees. Stir together flour, Parmesan, and paprika.

Dip potatoes in milk then dredge in flour mixture. Place potatoes on their sides into jelly roll pan and drizzle with butter.

Bake for 45 to 50 minutes, turning potatoes at half-way point during baking. Serve with sour cream and chives.

June 13-15, 1992

THANK YOU FOR SHARING YOUR HOME
WITH US. IT WAS A DELIGHTFUL STAY,
AND WOULD NOT HESITATE TO RETURN
IT WAS LIKE SLEEPING ON THE Pillsbury
DoughBoy. WELL WE MUST BE OFF,
BACK TO THE REAL World WHERE THIS
PLACE BECOMES A WONDERFUL MEMORY.

Tawcha & JERRY

7/11/92
y̓ᵉ Geᵒ Washington room
a pleasant respite
from the (domestic)
Battle of Brooklyn
Lee & Mike

Roasted Potatoes & Sausage
with a Goat Cheese & Herb Dressing

If you want to "dress" up your potatoes elegantly, this is for you.

1½ pounds sausage
2 pounds red potatoes

Dressing:
1 shallot
1 clove garlic
1 tablespoon parsley
1 tablespoon chives
1 teaspoon basil
1 teaspoon Dijon mustard
1 tablespoon lemon juice
3 tablespoons white wine vinegar
¾ cup olive oil
½ teaspoon salt
¼ teaspoon pepper
½ cup goat cheese, crumbled

Spray a roasting pan generously with non-stick cooking spray or coat with vegetable oil. Cut sausage and potatoes into bite size pieces and place in pan. Roast for 1 hour at 400 degrees or until sausage is fully cooked.

Meanwhile, prepare dressing:
Combine all dressing ingredients with a whisk. Pour dressing over potatoes and sausage; toss and serve.

Sept 28, 1992

Dear George —

    It was good to spend this short time with you. You are excellent company; your gaze is very .... presidential, your face is totally devoid of a smile, yet just as far from a frown; equanimity personified.
    And your feather bed! Fantastic!!

Dennis + Debbie

Helpful Hint: Our recipes calling for "baked and diced" potatoes, require baked and refrigerated cold potatoes. We keep a supply on hand at all times. It's a great way for you to use any extras from last night's dinner.

Curried Ham Potatoes

Serves 12

1 green pepper, diced
1 red pepper, diced
1 cup pineapple chunks (canned or fresh)
2 cups ham, cooked and diced
2 teaspoons curry
½ teaspoon cardamom
Salt and pepper
½ stick butter, melted
4 potatoes, baked and diced
1 teaspoon dry thyme

Combine all ingredients in a roasting pan. Roast at 400 degrees for 1 hour, stirring occasionally.

3·3·95

To George, Martha & the Kirbys,
        Our stay in your lovely
home made our first anniversary
absolutely DeLightful!! The breakfasts,
The Tea, the fun, and the use of
your pets were great! And - WOW -
we like feather beds!! We're already
making plans for our next stay and
you kNow we will tell all who'll listen
about the Sea Crest. We can't tell
you how wonderfull its been here
(and we know George won't!) Thank
you
(Martha & George   Mort & AnneMarie
will keep all our secrets)
        Bloomingdale
            NJ

72

Wild Mushroom Pasta

We like to prepare this recipe in three steps the day before serving.
When ready to bake, combine all the ingredients.

Serves 6

8 ounces pasta, cooked
12 ounces sliced mushrooms, any combination of the following
mushrooms (use at least two):
Porcini
Shitake
Button
Portabella
2 tablespoons olive oil
2 cloves garlic, crushed
2 tablespoons parsley

Béchamel sauce:
1 small onion stuck with 6 cloves
2½ cups milk
1 bay leaf
Nutmeg to taste
4 tablespoons melted butter
2 tablespoons flour
¼ cup Parmesan cheese

Spray a deep casserole type dish with non-stick cooking spray. Cook pasta according to package directions. We like tri-colored Fusilli for this dish. Sauté mushrooms in olive oil; add garlic and parsley.

Stick a small onion with cloves. Place in a saucepan with milk, bay leaf and nutmeg. Simmer for 45 minutes. Make a roux with butter and flour. Add to sauce at the end to thicken. Combine ingredients and pour into casserole dish; top with Parmesan cheese. Bake at 350 degrees until bubbling.

AUGUST 16, 1994

(TO THE TUNE OF GILLIGAN'S ISLAND)

NO PHONES, NO TUNES, NO T.V. SETS
JUST CENTURY OLD LUXURY —

LIKE ROBIN LEACH'S T.V. SHOW AS CLASSY
AS CAN BE —

WE'LL BE SURE TO JOIN CAROL AND JOHN HERE
AGAIN — BECAUSE YOU ALWAYS GET A SMILE —

FROM TWO ROMANTIC PARENTS ON A 5TH
ANNIVERSARY GETAWAY —

HERE IN THE ROOM WITH THE ROMANTIC REMOTE
CONTROLLED FIRE —

ANDY + RANDI
WAYNE, NJ

P.S. GEORGE'S EYES MOVE

Potatoes with Blue Cheese and Walnuts

A great recipe from "The Vegetarian Gourmet"

Serves 4

1 pound small new potatoes
4 stalks of celery, sliced
Small red onion, sliced
4 ounces blue cheese, mashed
½ cup light cream
Salt and ground black pepper
½ cup walnut pieces
2 tablespoons fresh parsley, chopped

Cover the potatoes with water and boil for about 15 minutes, adding the sliced celery and onion to the pan for the last 5 minutes or so.

Drain the vegetables and put them into a shallow serving dish.

In a small saucepan, melt the cheese in the cream, slowly, stirring occasionally. Do not allow the mixture to boil, but heat it until it scalds.

Season the sauce to taste. Pour over the vegetables and scatter over the walnuts and parsley. Serve hot.

MAY 1, 2   1996

George,
    Having had many overnights this
past year, there is something
wonderful about feeling like you're
home when you are not. I
felt like I have been here many
times before (and I hope to
be here again).
    I sit here, the morning of my
15th wedding anniversary, without
my wife, Maryann, as I'm on
a business trip and realize
that is what is missing! If
you could have produced her, it
would have been a perfect stay.
    This, now, leaves me the
opportunity to return and enjoy
Sea Gest even more! Thank You!

                    Kevin
                    Hamilton N.J.
I'm running for US Congress in the 4th
DISTRICT, SPRING LAKE HTS is as close as
my district comes. See you soon!

76

Jersey Shore Potatoes

We make these potatoes for our July 4ᵗʰ celebration.
They take you back to your childhood
when Mom made "comfort food."

Serves 12

6-8 potatoes, baked, cooled and sliced
1 pound Taylor ham, sliced (any good baked ham will work well)
1 recipe white sauce (see recipe on page 159)
1 cup grated cheddar cheese

Layer potatoes, ham and cheese in large baking dish. Cover with white sauce and bake in 350 degree oven until bubbling.

Sept 15, 1997

Well it is almost official. I came here with my lover to celebrate my divorce. After ten years of being stuck in a marriage I am finally free to get away w/ Jack without all the cloak and dagger. Two years ago I met Jack on a business trip and since then we have only been able to see each other when my "ex" husband was away. Although at first I believed that our affair was caused in the thrill of "cheating," I soon found myself falling in love with him and out of love with my husband. I know I should not have had an affair in the first place but I am fairly certain now that I never really loved my husband. I am finally free to say what has been in my heart for years. I Love You Jack. And I don't care who knows it!

Carolyn

Potato Pancakes
(Not Latkes)

4 large potatoes, baked and diced
½ cup cooked and crumbled bacon
⅓ cup dried onion bits
½ cup sour cream
2 eggs
¼ cup milk
Salt and pepper
1 teaspoon garlic powder

Combine potatoes, bacon, onion, sour cream, eggs, milk, salt and pepper, and garlic powder in mixer and blend, or process as you would mashed potatoes.

Heat a griddle or pan (cast iron preferred) to medium-high heat. Butter pan and place large spoonfuls of potatoes onto griddle, carefully pressing into pancakes (hands work best). Cook 5 to 7 minutes on each side until golden brown. Serve with sour cream with chives and applesauce.

Your Inn is quite
lovely but it is a
shame that your staff
is so unpleasant.
Barbara & Joe Siehr

9/26 – 28/97
Great sunrises and great Service!
We enjoyed our stay tremendously
and look forward to returning
soon.
Thanks Bill + Mary
Wallingford, CT

Rosemary Potatoes with Sausage

Serves 12 - 15

12 medium red potatoes, diced
1 large onion, sliced
3 apples, diced
1 pound sweet Italian sausage, cut into bite-size pieces
Salt and pepper
3 tablespoons garlic, minced
3 tablespoons dry rosemary or 3-4 fresh sprigs
1 stick butter

Combine potatoes, onion, apples, sausage, salt and pepper, garlic, rosemary, and butter. Roast at 400 degrees for 2 hours. If you prepare a day ahead, roast for 90 minutes then heat at 400 degrees for 90 minutes the next morning.

Southwest Potatoes with Ham

1 pound diced honeybaked Virginia ham
1 cup diced green pepper
1 cup diced red pepper
1 large onion, diced
Salt and pepper to taste

Combine ham, peppers, onions. Salt and pepper to taste. Roast at 400 degrees for 2 hours.

15-November-97

A Perfect Place To "Regroup." Thank You For An Opportunity To Recover From A Hectic, But Wonderful, Year (Married, New Home, Birth Of Our First Very Special Child!) And A Chance To Prepare Ourselves For The Fast Approaching Holidays. The B&B Is A Great Touch, If Not Only A Great Pun! It's Comforting Effect Goes All The Way Back To Teething (A Little On The Gums)

To The Staff, Keepers, Owners - Much Joy, Peace & Good Health!

To Those That Follow In Our Steps - Remember The Irish Phylosophy (And Ignore My Spelling!):

In This World, There Are Only Two Things To Worry About; Health Or Sickness. If You Are Well, No Worries. If You Are Ill...

You Will Get Better, Or You Will Die. If You Get Well, No Worries. If You Die...

Heaven Or Hell. If You Go To Heaven, No Worries. If You Go To Hell, You're To Busy Shaking Hands W/ Old Friends To Worry.

So, The Moral Is There Is Not Much You Can't Make The Best Of, So No Worries

Isabel & Andrew
Baltimore, Maryland

Iz & Dru Slept Here!

82

Diaries from

Key to the Bread Machine

—The Diaries of Pussy Willow—
Some would claim this room, that is little bigger than a bread box,
is the Old Lady's most comfortable.
Actually, it is Carol's favorite because she can lay in bed
and watch the ocean and it has a big tub.

8-90   they say cats have nine lives. Our first life in "Pussy Willow" was filled with love & romance. My beau said "marry me" and that's just what I'm going to do! that way we can have 8 more lives in "Pussy Willo" and then try the "Mard Gras"
        Cindi & Paul

Lovely Eileen, with your elegant black gloves and ruby lips; Pussy Willow brought out the best of your feline graces. I wish that we humans, like cats, had nine lives so I could spend my other eight and a half around you. Sea Crest will always carry thoughts of a beautiful end of our first year. I'd love to come back, to the same gracious host and their marvelous breakfast, and with the same beautiful companion   1/9/90

Our bread recipes are for a 1° pound loaf. They should be put into the machine in the order listed. If your machine instructions are to add dry ingredients first, just make the recipe backwards. We have tried them both ways with equal results, as long as the yeast stays dry.
Use the "basic bread" setting for all recipes.

Cottage Dill Bread

¾ cup water
3 cups bread flour
1½ tablespoons dry milk
2 tablespoons sugar
1½ teaspoons salt
1½ tablespoons butter
¾ cup cottage cheese
1 tablespoon dry onion
1 tablespoon dill weed
1 tablespoon dill seed
3 teaspoons yeast

Bake on "basic bread" setting.

5/19/91

WOULDN'T IT BE NICE TO
LIVE LIFE LIKE A CAT?
TO HAVE SOMEBODY FEED YOU,
CHANG YOUR WATER, LITTER
TO NOT HAVE TO WORK AND TO
BE ABLE TO SLEEP ALL DAY
BUT WHEN I LOOK OUT THE
WINDOW, TOWARDS THE OCEAN
I REALIZE HOW MUCH MORE
FREEDOM I HAVE THAN A CAT
WHO IS USUALLY CONFINED TO A
NEIGHBORHOOD AND SOMETIMES A HOUSE
BECAUSE I ~~HAVE AM~~ FREE, I FOUND
~~THE~~ ONE I LOVE
BUT IT IS HERE, THIS WEEKEND,
WHERE WE COULD ACT LIKE
TWO CATS IN LOVE.
                    BRUNO

Sally Lunn

A special favorite of Jeanne and Robert. Also known as "Dirty Lady Bread." As the story goes, in Merry Old England, "Sally made and sold bread instead of herself."

$\frac{1}{4}$ cup milk
$\frac{1}{2}$ cup water
7 tablespoons butter
3 eggs
1$\frac{1}{2}$ teaspoons salt
$\frac{1}{4}$ cup sugar
3 cups bread flour
2 teaspoons yeast

Assemble ingredients in bread machine in order listed. Bake on "basic bread" setting.

Honey Walnut Bread

1$\frac{1}{4}$ cups water
1$\frac{1}{2}$ cups bread flour
1$\frac{1}{2}$ cups whole wheat flour
3 tablespoons honey
1$\frac{1}{2}$ teaspoons salt
2 tablespoons butter
3 teaspoons yeast
$\frac{1}{2}$ cup walnuts

Assemble ingredients in bread machine in order listed. Bake on "basic bread" setting.

6/10/91

It was wonderful
watching the sunrise
over the Atlantic while
lying in bed.
And "The Diary of a Cat"
is a classic.
Mostly, we will remember
the Pussy Willow room
and the jelly bean.

Don't ask.

Bob & Robin

Bob is being a wise guy. I told
him not to write about the jellybean.
I choked on one & came dangerously
close to going to cat heaven. After
all was said & done I decided if it
had to happen, this was a wonderful
spot.   Robin

Rueben
he's got
very big
feet

these are our
2 cats

Ruby Red lips

88

Old Fashioned Oatmeal Bread

1 cup water
$\frac{1}{4}$ cup molasses
2 tablespoons butter
3 cups bread flour
$\frac{1}{2}$ cup quick or regular oats
2 tablespoons dry milk
$1\frac{1}{4}$ teaspoons salt
3 teaspoons yeast

Assemble ingredients in bread machine in order listed. Bake on "basic bread" setting.

Honey Mustard Bread

$1\frac{1}{4}$ cups hot water
1 bouillon cube
2 cups bread flour
1 cup wheat flour
1 tablespoon dry milk
$\frac{1}{4}$ cup honey
1 teaspoon salt
$2\frac{1}{2}$ tablespoons Dijon mustard
2 teaspoons chives
3 teaspoons yeast

Dissolve bouillon cube in hot water; let cool. Assemble ingredients in bread machine in order listed. Bake on "basic bread" setting.

Hicory-Dicory-Dock Mouse Happy

Man, there are a lot of clocks in this town. There's even a store where the clocks are so expensive that nobody can afford them.

Nobody in this town must ever have to ask what time it is. Except for the good ol' boys who hang around the filling station. And they love to catch some thinking person with the question, "do you know what time it is?" Then they damn near hurt themselves guffawing and slapping their thighs.

The last person to actually ask someone what time it was was Shorty Evans. It was on April 11, 1955, the same day one Alfred Smith of Durbin, Australia caught a 16 foot 9 inch 2536 pound Great White Shark with a rod and reel. But that's another story all together.

So, it's April 11, 1955, 12:15 PM, and Shorty's mother has just baked a chocolate cake. Shorty asks his grandfather what time it is. He doesn't just ask once, but he asks 232 times. Shortly after shorty was committed to the state mental Facilities.

But it's O.K., because For Short every day is April 11, 1955, 12:15 PM and his mother has just baked a chocolate cake. Shorty is happy.

There are many clocks here at Sea Crest by the Sea too. So many clocks that all of the cats that adorn this room must be Hicory- Dicory - Dock Mouse happy.

Richard
10:13 PM

8/11/93

FANTASTIC! ESPECIALLY OUR
TANDEM BIKE RIDE THROUGH SPRING
LAKE. SAD OVER THE MONMOUTH
HOTEL'S FATE. BUT MOSTLY SPRING
LAKE REMAINS AS IT DID IN
1964, WHEN I STAYED HERE
ALL SUMMER AS A YOUNG 7
YEAR OLD. THE "SEA CREST" IS
ABSOLUTELY ..... WONDERFUL. OUR
TWO DAY STAY HERE HAS
HELPED US REGAIN FAITH AND
ALOT OF HOPE IN OUR YOUNG
RELATIONSHIP. I AM "IN LOVE"
FOR THE 1ST TIME SINCE
GETTING INTO RECOVERY. THE
"PUSSYWILLOW" IS SO RELAXING.
WE MADE FABULOUS LOVE
ATOP A MOUNTAIN OF SOFT
SHEETS AND PILLOWS. HOPE
TO RETURN IN WINTER.

PETE   PRINCETON
N.J

I can't believe he wrote that!
I'm so embarassed! Pete

92

Olive Bread

1¼ cups water
2 tablespoons olive oil
3¼ cups bread flour
½ tablespoon sugar
1 teaspoon salt
1½ tablespoons dry milk
½ cup black olives, whole or sliced
2 teaspoons basil
1 teaspoon garlic powder
3 teaspoons yeast

Assemble ingredients in bread machine in order listed. Bake on "basic bread" setting.

Pumpernickel Bread

1 cup plus 2 tablespoons water
¼ cup dark molasses
1 tablespoon butter
2 cups bread flour
1¼ cups rye flour
2 tablespoons cocoa powder
2 teaspoons salt
3½ teaspoons yeast

Assemble ingredients in bread machine in order listed. Bake on "basic bread" setting.

9-30 — 10-3 '93
Pussy
Willows

A lovely
visit among
lovely things!
Especially en-
joyed seeing
the sun rise
without having
to get out of
bed!!
Looking fo-
ward to my
next visit ~

MARITA

94

Potato Bread

1¼ cups water
2 tablespoons butter
3¼ cups bread flour
½ cup mashed potato mix
1 tablespoon sugar
1½ teaspoons salt
3 teaspoons yeast

Assemble ingredients in bread machine in order listed. Bake on "basic bread" setting.

Tomato Basil Bread

1¼ cups water
1 tablespoon butter
2 teaspoons chopped garlic
3¼ cups bread flour
¼ cup Parmesan cheese
2 tablespoons sugar
1½ teaspoons salt
1½ teaspoons dry basil
⅓ cup chopped sun-dried tomatoes
3 teaspoons yeast

Assemble ingredients in bread machine in order listed. Bake on "basic bread" setting.

We know a little pussy,
her coat is soft & gray,
She lives down in the meadow
not very far away —
She'll always be a pussy,
she'll never be a cat,
'cause she's a Pussy Willow,
now what do you think of that
Meow, meow, meow —
                    Scat

Our stay was lovely —
restful. The only call
out of our comfy bed was
the tantalizing aroma drifting
under the door.
    Food and conversation
was a delight for body
and soul.
        Thank you for your
efforts to make our stay
so memorable.
            Joe & Dixie

THANK'S MUCH! :)

June 10th 1994

We had a wonderfull and Marvlous time in your Beautiful sweet Home. The Breakfast was ummm! — Delicious!

Thank's for everything...
We'll short be back soon!

Jaima, Ana + Frank!

We Loved!
We loved!
We loved!
We Loved!
We loved!
we Loved!
We Loved!
we Loved!
we Loved!
we Loved!
It was Great!

October 29, 1994

The house is beautiful and we love the location. Thanks for adequate parking, an excellent bed (especially the comforter) and the Caswell-Massey toiletries. Breakfasts were scrumptious and we appreciated the afternoon tea. Thank you for "no kids and no smoking." We only wish there were not so many nick-nacks and souvenirs/decor on the surfaces of tables + dressers, as we guests need places to put our things. Please consider polyurethane-ing the wooden surfaces in the bathrooms, as they are not practical in such a watery locale. Again, more cleared space there would have been preferable. I wish you didn't have cats, but as cats go, yours are quite sweet. A worthwhile stay,

N. + R.
PA

Cheddar Chive Bread

$1\frac{1}{4}$ cups water
$3\frac{1}{4}$ cups bread flour
$1\frac{1}{4}$ cups shredded cheddar cheese
$\frac{1}{4}$ cup fresh chives
2 tablespoons sugar
$\frac{3}{4}$ teaspoon salt
3 teaspoons yeast

Assemble ingredients in bread machine in order listed. Bake on "basic bread" setting.

Cinnamon Raisin Bread

Great for Rum Raisin French Toast

$1\frac{1}{4}$ cups water
2 tablespoons butter
$3\frac{1}{4}$ cups bread flour
$\frac{1}{4}$ cup sugar
$1\frac{1}{2}$ teaspoons salt
1 teaspoon cinnamon
3 teaspoons yeast
$\frac{3}{4}$ cup raisins

Assemble ingredients in bread machine in order listed. Bake on "basic bread" setting.

9 May 1997

God is in the details - like the swan using
its beak to gently rearrange the eggs in the nest
for a better fit and the many beautiful ways
you think of to make this house comfortable
for us. A carefully constructed nest is an
apt image for this weekend. It's our second
trip and our relationship has grown -
so has Sea Crest and Spring Lake. There
are new houses and a new boardwalk.
We rode to the lake on new bicycles.
The ocean is old and new both - its
power irresistible. This time we saw
and felt it in rain and wind as well
as sun. Your breakfasts nourished
us all day. We are already planning
what to eat for dinner when we come
back. Our cat commends you on your
choice of decor (we stayed in Pussy
Willow).

Sharon

Lemon Poppy Seed Bread

3/4 cup water
3 cups bread flour
1 1/2 tablespoons dry milk
1 teaspoon salt
1 1/2 tablespoons butter
3/4 cup lemon yogurt
2 tablespoons honey
1/2 cup almonds, chopped
1 tablespoon lemon peel
3 tablespoons poppy seeds
2 teaspoons lemon extract
3 teaspoons yeast

Assemble ingredients in bread machine in order listed. Bake on "basic bread" setting.

Parmesan Pepper Bread

1 cup plus 2 tablespoons water
1 tablespoon olive oil
3 1/4 cups bread flour
1/2 cup Parmesan cheese
1 tablespoon sugar
1 teaspoon salt
3/4 teaspoon fresh ground black pepper
3 teaspoons yeast

Assemble ingredients in bread machine in order listed. Bake on "basic bread" setting.

"Pussy Willow Room"

Sept. 14, 199-

Dear Carol & John

I would like to express my gratitude for your most hospitable & caring way you received me. May God Bless you both. It was a privilege to know such a sweet couple!. I enjoyed my week here, only thing it went too fast but with the help of "God" I'd like to return this coming summer again.

Your staff are also the best you could employ nothing was too much for Terry to do, to arrange where I would eat every evening, she was so concerned, I Love her; and love you all.

"God Bless"
Dorothy

P.S. Lets us not forget the delicious food you served. It really tickled my palate & my tummy, liked it too. (It shows) HA,

Diaries from

Queen
Victoria

Key to Muffins

—The Diaries from Queen Victoria—
The Young Queen in all her glory.
Don't miss the entry from September 15th, 1996 on
the birth of Winnie, Minnie, and Ginnie. Quack!

10/27/95   10/28/95

As a special gift from
our children, we are
able to spend our
45th Anniversary here.
Its by far the
loveliest place we have
ever stayed at.
          Hope to be able to
come back soon.

                    Joe & Fran Kuzezyk

11/3/95 - 11/4/95

Ours is a storybook romance
poetically written. This
weekend we celebrated
a year in finding one
another as well as
Randy's birthday. The
Queen Victoria is
very romantic and added

to the memories we've
made this last year.

This weekend we spent
many hours just talking
and spending wonderful
quality time together.
This beautiful suite
gave us privacy and
peacefulness. We are
leaving with much
contentment and
a little more love
than we arrived with –
for each time we're
together our love grows.

Thank you for allowing
us to share your
home and hospitality.
I can't wait to
come back.
Terry

4/5/98

Finding the love in my life came 10 years ago. We met, shared time together, then unfortunately did not see each other for 5 years. Life did not allow us to be together as we'd like, so for 4 more years we could only share brief encounters. Always protecting ourselves and all around us. We feared we'd never share our love as two people who feel the way we do should. Finally Nov 2 1994 we gave all there is to give to one another. Since that time we have taken time out for only the two of us. Always special always memorable. Spending the weekend with my Queen in your Queens suite has been a most memorable weekend. I'm grateful to have had the chance to share my heart felt feelings with Terry and you John & Carol. I hope to return someday unfeel unfeel as we both desire somuch. Your warm and friendly atmosphere makes enjoying the love of my life very special.

R

10/9/45

After this last passage, I am left to fully speachless.

Are these people married? Are they having an affair?

Are they my Relatives? My wife's Relatives?

We're having fun and that's all that really matters.

4/21/96

    4-19 the day we
arrived was a lucky
number for 4 reasons:
  ① married 19 years
  ② our address is 19
  ③ the date is the 19th
  ④ and of course the
  address here is 19.

    Believe it or not, we
did not realize this until
the evening of the 19th. And,
oh, by the way my
birthday is 8/19. Alex
aid a lovely, relaxing
weekend we will always
remember.
          Joanne & Bob

108

Some say muffins are passe, we disagree. There is always room for muffins on your table and on your plate. Whether they are mini, maxi, crumbly, crunchy or filled, it doesn't matter. Here are some of our favorites.

Blueberry Crunch Muffins

Yield: 18 muffins

Muffins:
¼ cup butter or margarine
¾ cup sugar
1 egg
2 cups all-purpose flour
½ teaspoon salt
2 teaspoons baking powder
½ cup milk
2 cups blueberries, washed and drained

For muffins:
Cream butter, and sugar. Add egg and mix well. Sift flour, salt, and baking powder together. Add to the creamed mixture with the milk, mixing only until ingredients are moistened. Gently fold in berries. Divide batter into 18 muffin cups, either greased on lined with paper baking cups.

Topping:
½ cup sugar
⅓ cup all-purpose flour
½ teaspoon cinnamon
½ teaspoon nutmeg
¼ cup butter or margarine, softened

For topping:
Combine ingredients with a fork to make a crumbly mixture. Sprinkle on top of muffin batter. Bake at 375 degrees for 15 to 20 minutes.

Lemon Yogurt Muffins

One of the first muffins from the Sea Crest kitchen, this winner is still talked about today by innkeeper Art. He was overcome by these tangy, not too sweet muffins, over 8 years ago!

Yield: 12 muffins

2 cups all-purpose flour
1 teaspoon baking powder
1 teaspoon baking soda
¼ teaspoon salt
¼ cup sugar
2 tablespoons honey
2 eggs
1¼ cups plain or lemon yogurt
¼ cup (½ stick) butter, melted
1 tablespoon grated lemon zest

Lemon syrup:
⅓ cup lemon juice
⅓ cup sugar
3 tablespoons water

Preheat oven to 375 degrees and butter muffin tins.

In a small bowl, blend together the flour, baking powder, baking soda, and salt. In another bowl, combine the sugar, honey, eggs, yogurt, melted butter, and lemon zest and beat until thoroughly mixed. Add the combined dry ingredients and beat until just blended.

Spoon the batter into the prepared muffin tins, filling each cup about two-thirds full. Bake for 15 minutes or until the tops are delicately browned and toothpick or straw inserted into the center of a muffin comes out clean.

While the muffins bake, prepare the syrup: Combine the lemon juice, sugar and water in small saucepan. Bring to a boil. Boil for 1 minute; set aside.

When the muffins are done, remove the pan from the oven and cool on wire rack. Gently poke holes in muffin tops with a large tined fork and drizzle lemon mixture over tops.

TUESDAY JUNE 18, 1996

I REALLY FEEL LIKE THIS
IS MY FANTASY HOME.
WHERE ONLY GOOD CAN
HAPPEN TO ME AND IT HAS.
I CAN TOTALLY RELAX AND
REJUVINATE MY SPIRIT.
IT ALSO REMINDS ME OF
MY GRANDPARENTS WHO I
STILL MISS SINCE THEY
PASSED ON OVER 40 YEARS
AGO.
ON A LIGHTER NOTE ....
I LOVE THE RUBBER DUCK!
I DON'T REMEMBER EVER
HAVING ONE IN MY BATH.
THANK GOD FOR HELPING
YOU TO PROVIDE SUCH A
DELIGHTFUL DEPARTURE
FROM REALITY.

LOVE
BMW

Raspberry Chocolate Chip Muffins

Fabulous anytime. In summer we use John's fresh picked raspberries, but in winter frozen raspberries work well too.

Yield: 12 muffins

2 cups all-purpose flour
$1/4$ to $1/2$ cup sugar to taste
$2^1/2$ teaspoons baking powder
$1/2$ teaspoon salt
$1/4$ teaspoon nutmeg
1 cup milk
$1/2$ cup butter, melted and cooled
1 egg, slightly beaten
1 cup raspberries
$1/4$ cup mini chocolate chips

Preheat oven to 400 degrees. Grease 12 muffin cups.

In a large bowl, stir together flour, sugar, baking powder, salt, and nutmeg. In another bowl, combine milk, butter, and egg. Make a well in the middle of the dry ingredients and add butter mixture; stir just until combined. Stir in berries and chocolate chips with just a few additional strokes.

Bake 20 to 30 minutes, or until cake tester comes out clean. Cool 5 minutes and remove muffins to wire rack to finish cooling. For a nice touch, dust with powdered sugar before serving.

Cappuccino Chip Muffins

Yield: 12 muffins

2 cups all-purpose flour
¾ cup sugar
2½ teaspoons baking powder
2 teaspoons instant espresso coffee powder
½ teaspoon salt
½ teaspoon ground cinnamon
1 cup half-and-half
½ cup lightly salted butter or margarine, melted and cooled
1 egg, lightly beaten
1 teaspoon vanilla
¾ cup semi-sweet chocolate mini chips

Preheat oven to 375 degrees. Grease twelve 3 x 1¼-inch (3½- to 4-ounce) muffin cups.

In a large bowl, stir together flour, sugar, baking powder, espresso coffee powder, salt, and cinnamon. In another bowl, stir together milk, butter, egg, and vanilla until blended. Make a well in center of dry ingredients; add milk mixture and stir just to combine. Stir in chips.

Spoon batter into prepared muffin cups; bake 15 to 20 minutes or until a cake tester inserted in center comes out clean.

Remove muffin tin or tins to wire rack. Cool 5 minutes before removing muffins from cups; finish cooling on rack. Serve warm or cool completely and store in airtight container at room temperature.

The muffins freeze well.

September 15, 1996
In here today with my best friend and lover Maryellen to rejuvinate our love for each other. This is our 3rd time here and as always we love the Sea Crest + this room. During the day I deliver babies and I turned off me beeper to get away from "the baby business." HOWEVER — — — when we were enjoying the jacuzzi + each other (if you know what I mean) I heard a blood curdling QUACK!!! → The rubber duckie was in labor. Needless to say Maryellen + I knew what we had to do — — So we got the towels + hot water — — — I washed my hands and we were ready — — —> next page — >

sh...

114

I would have rolled
up my sleeves but
I was naked.
    after I showed her
how to push out the
3 eggs + we waited
and watched all night
until Winnie, Minnie,
and Ginnie were
hatched.. What a
night — I think I
should get a discount
on the room for having
to go to work while
on vacation!!!
    Anyway we had a
wonderful time — the
breakfast I'm sure
would have been "to
die for" but we had
to BOLT at 7³⁰A.
Hope to be back soon + see
the 3 little duckies
all grown up!   Charles

~~~ Sept 22, 1996

Well, I arrived today w/o my wife -- who has to work midnights tonight. I'll pick her up in the morning.

I just spent the last 40 minutes in the jacuzzi reading, followed by some quality time by myself reading in the sitting room. I could get use to this!

Sept. 24.

Last year my husband & I celebrated our 1st year anniversary here in the Teddy Roosevelt room. We both thought everything was fantastic. This year as we celebrated our 2nd year anniversary in the Queen Victoria Suite I have a much different outlook. The sitting area was very nice. You could really lounge - much more

We home. The bath room was biggg
the tub was nice. (I needed cool
water, since I have low blood pressure
and with very warm water I felt
faint)

* Also, a quick ridiculous note *
Don't put the jets on until the
water is way above the jets. I
was not that fortunate or smart.
I sat in the tub turned on the
jets and literally was in a
high speed car wash. Was pretty
funny though!

The bedroom I did not like at
all. Too much furniture and
too big. I felt very cramped.
The bed was way too high,
way too soft to be inviting.
You had to pole vault up there
and once there I felt like I was
laying on a pile of folded clothes

in a clothes basket. Also, the way the mattress does not meet the head board gave me the feeling I was on a pull-out sofa (room above you head.)

On the second night I slept out in the sitting room on the cushions from the wicker couch.

This was even after my husband took out the feather ↴

On the eating note. I really do enjoy the breakfasts, but, I did not sleep w/ these people and my husband and I did not come here to make soul mates w/ people eating scones beside us. I really do not like the continued conversation that tends to go on at the table. We tried to eat at the small table for two so as not to be disturbed. I mean we were on a romantic weekend, not a convention. Also, some people don't have really good table manners. Something is wrong w/ this picture — when you're eating a beautifully prepared + served breakfast on China and somebody is chewing w/ their mouth open, slurping or sucking their teeth. No, we did not come here for that. In fact, every place we went to eat, we also were real "pigs in the 'trough'"

The last night we were out (the menus decided were to go and 4 people came in and inquired about "where + what + when did you" questions, so my husband (and) obliged and answered them and was quite congenial. In came the husband of one of these women was chewing gum like and over-sized piece of fat back, keeping both lips open so it could echo w/ every word he was trying to pronounce.

Don't people or the other people realize that you're ~~supposed to~~ not supposed to eat like this.

Well, at the conculsion of my trip I have realized alot. This trip reaffirmed my love for antiques, which we spent most of our time perusing the shops.

I miss our bed very much. and as much as I thought it was a bad quality I love the company of my husband entirely, ~~don't feel~~ the least bit unsociable not talking w/ these strangers. My husband and I are at best two sorts of the same mirror or at least two different mirrors which can share at the same thing at the same time. It's a rare thing when we are opposingly opposed to any event, manners, idea etc. So I have been appreciated my view. And I'm sure this will endure for the rest of our lives.

Jon & Chuck

October 5, 1996

Queen Victoria never had it this good. A wonderful adventure on a 42 year journey.

Dick & Jean
Pottstown Pa

P.S. - It would be nice if you would train Winnie, Minnie, & Ginnie not to jump into the jacuzzi when others are using it, five in the tub is just too many! Thank you John & Carol for providing such a beautiful haven for others to enjoy!

Jean

12/96

Veni, vidi, Ginnie, Winnie Minnie.
We came, we saw, we played with the ducks.
Relax t enjoy.
                         K+S

             August 19th

Love comes from years
of breathing
skin to skin
tangled in each other's dreams
until each night weaves
weaves another thread
in the same web
of blood + sleep

and I have only
passed through you quickly
like light

and you have only
surrounded me suddenly
like flame'
                         Mary

    We had a wonderful time and truly
enjoyed an intimate getaway. for our
23rd Anniv.

Sea Crest Buttermilk Scones

Our signature scone is available in our gift shop for guests who want to take a little of the Sea Crest home with them.

Yield: 8 scones

2 cups all-purpose flour
$\frac{1}{3}$ cup granulated sugar
$1\frac{1}{2}$ teaspoons baking powder
$\frac{1}{2}$ teaspoon baking soda
$\frac{1}{4}$ teaspoon salt
6 tablespoons unsalted butter, chilled
$\frac{1}{2}$ cup buttermilk
1 large egg
$1\frac{1}{2}$ teaspoons vanilla extract
$\frac{2}{3}$ cup currant or raisins (optional)

Preheat oven to 400 degrees. In a large bowl, stir together flour, sugar, baking powder, baking soda, and salt. Cut the butter into $\frac{1}{2}$-inch cubes and distribute them over the flour mixture. With a pastry blender or two knives used scissors fashion, cut in the butter until the mixture resembles coarse crumbs. In a small bowl, stir together the buttermilk, egg, and vanilla. Add the buttermilk mixture to the flour mixture and stir to combine. Stir in the currants or raisins, if desired.

With lightly floured hands, pat the dough into an 8-inch diameter circle on an ungreased baking sheet. With a serrated knife, cut into 8 wedges. Bake for 18 to 20 minutes, or until the top is lightly browned and a cake tester or toothpick inserted into center of scone comes out clean.

Remove the baking sheet to a wire rack and cool for 5 minutes. Using a spatula, transfer the scones to the wire rack to cool. Recut into wedges if necessary. Serve warm or cool completely and store in an airtight container.

Orange Butterscotch Muffins

These will remind you of the muffins you had as a child at Aunt Fanny's house.

Yield: 12 muffins

1 cup sugar
1 stick butter, softened
2 large eggs
Grated peel of 2 medium oranges
½ cup plain yogurt or buttermilk
½ cup fresh orange juice
1 teaspoon baking powder
½ teaspoon baking soda
2 cups flour
¾ cup butterscotch chips

Preheat oven to 350 degrees. Grease muffin cups.

Cream sugar and butter; beat in eggs, one at a time, and add orange peel. Add yogurt, orange juice, baking powder, baking soda, and flour. Mix very well.

Add flour and butterscotch chips; mix until just blended. Pour into prepared cups and bake 15 to 20 minutes.

Aug 20 1997

A year ago (or there
abouts) I married
my best friend. We
met in the fall of
'82' at work, dated
a few months & then
lost touch for about
a year. I married
another but soon
to come to my ~~sens~~
senses and end that
hell to go to heaven
with my present love.
13 years later I know
"this is the real thing.
Still crazy after all
these years"
Y.T.
B.T. Rockland
New York

Yes, it's All TRUE! WE'VE HAD
MORE UPS & DOWNS THAN THE SWISS
ALPS :) BUT I would not BE the
PERSON THAT I AM TODAY without
my lovely wife.

125

...we had a wonderful breakfast. French Toast, potatoes, cobbler, fruit etc. Truly delicious. Then we took a bike ride around town & compared some B+B's to the Sea Crest. From the one's that we had seen, There is really no comparision. We Truly Lucked out with John & Carol's, Art & Terri's splendid B+B.

Sometimes Life passes by so quickly .... Like Lines on a Highway. So it's moments like these that are so truly Rewarding. It was nice to once again reach the level of love that we share. A Level that goes by unnoticed while tending to the business of life. Cherished moments experienced..... Like knowing what the other is thinking without saying a word ... Like the subtle touch of one's skin upon the other's...... Like lying in the arms of your lover

...and feel the warmth and security that can only come with the undying love shared.

This is a special place and time for me. It was time once again to feed the soul, to nourish the heart, to feel the love that only my wife can give me....

A love that I have NEVER KNOWN before, and a love that I will Never feel with another.!

Billy Rockland N.

P.S.
Long Live The Queen!!

Chocolate Cheesecake Muffins

Yield: 20 muffins

3-ounce package cream cheese
2 tablespoons sugar
1 cup all-purpose flour
½ cup sugar
3 tablespoons unsweetened cocoa powder
2 teaspoons baking powder
½ teaspoon salt
1 beaten egg
¾ cup milk
⅓ cup vegetable oil
Confectioners' sugar

Preheat oven to 375 degrees. In a small bowl, beat cream cheese and 2 tablespoons sugar until light and fluffy; set aside.

In a large bowl, stir together flour, ½ cup sugar, cocoa, baking powder, and salt. Make a well in center of dry ingredients. Combine egg, milk, and oil. Add all at once to dry ingredients, stirring until just moistened (batter should be lumpy). Spoon about 2 tablespoons of batter into greased muffin cups. Drop 1 teaspoon of cream cheese mixture on top and cover with more chocolate batter. Bake for 20 minutes. Dust with confectioners' sugar when cool.

Diaries from

Key to Strudels

—The Diaries from Teddy Roosevelt—
Teddy Roosevelt was the only Victorian President,
which is why we pay homage to him with our "Presidential" Suite.
The two rooms which his suite occupy are filled to the brim
with happy teddies. Victorian elegance and cuddly bears combined,
make this room a favorite for "childhood" sweethearts.

October 20, 1991

Enjoyed the company of the Bears!
Thank you for a wonderful week-end and for providing such a warm & lovely setting to relax in!

Marita

Feb 16, 1992

To John & Carol,
Thanks for a lovely time & the feeling of being pampered as guests of friends. Here's an old teddy bear poem for your room:

"My Teddy Bear" by Marchette Chute
A teddy bear is a faithful friend,
You can pick him up at either end.
His fur is the color of breakfast toast.
And he's always there when you need him most.

Joe & Lynn
West New York, N.J.

June 27, 1992

A great room to "hibernate" in for the weekend -- without the Cubs! Cannot bear to leave this romantic den - Looking forward to a return visit!

Mary Ellen & Dan

7/12/93

Needed to recoup + regroup - couldn't have found a better place! Splendid breakfasts, comfy bed (with a terrific reading lamp! So rare!) quiet little porch and of course that great boardwalk. Thank you!

Diane

P.S. Bears were most understanding & sincere - except for a few that got rowdy after midnight!

We really enjoyed
our First Anniversary bathing
and watching movies rented
from Blockbuster Video. We
were a little startled by
someone looking in from
the porch while we were
making love!! "Just a little
story to always remember
Sea Crest by the Sea."

Oct 17, 1993
Gay; Don

JANUARY 25 '94

Thank you for providing the
Ultimate hide-a-way for
two secret lovers ...
Everything was JUST DREAM-y;
almost can't BEAR to leave!
L.DuR & M.DA.
(P.S. We'll take along with
us some warm & squishy
memories, if you don't mind

○ L. DuR. Loves M. DA. 47 ª

I AM IN love & will be FOREVER
with L. DuR.

M . DA

132

Apple Strudel

Yield: 2 strudels

1 stick of butter
4 apples, diced
¼ cup lemon juice
½ cup brown sugar
1 teaspoon cinnamon
2 teaspoons vanilla
8 sheets filo dough
¼ cup sugar for sprinkling on top

Melt ½ stick butter in large skillet. Sprinkle apples with lemon juice to prevent discoloration. Add apples and simmer 10 to 15 minutes. Add the brown sugar, cinnamon, and vanilla. Stir until sugar is dissolved. Simmer 5 to 10 minutes more until the mixture thickens. Cool the mixture.

Melt the remaining ½ stick of butter. Place 2 sheets of filo dough down and brush with the butter. Then add 2 more sheets, brushing with the butter again. Spread half of the filling on the long side of the dough and carefully roll up. Brush the top with butter and sprinkle with sugar. Repeat for the second strudel. Bake 15 to 20 minutes at 350 degrees until golden.

Apple Sausage Strudel

Yield: 2 strudels

½ pound bulk sausage
2 apples, diced
1 sprig fresh rosemary
8 sheets of filo dough
½ stick of butter, melted

Cook the sausage in a large skillet over medium heat. Dice the apples and add to the sausage. Add the rosemary. Lower heat and simmer until the apples are soft. Cool and remove the rosemary. Follow assembly instructions for the Apple Strudel (recipe above).

2 March '94

We're sure that the bears are discreet... It's that rubber ducky we're concerned about. He never stopped grinning.

This was our first – it won't be our last and we travel all the way from Monasquon.

We've stayed at B & B's for years – this is the best. Keep up the good work & let us know if you ever want to sell.

Joe & Joni

July 4, 1994

Thank-you for a wonderful and relaxing week-end. The bed was so inviting, while the bath was so exciting...

Patty and Tony
♥

134

Brie and Mushroom Strudel

Serves 6

1½ cups sliced mushrooms
1 tablespoon butter
1 tablespoon dry sherry
1 teaspoon Worcestershire
¼ teaspoon thyme
Black pepper
4 sheets filo dough
3 - 4 tablespoons melted butter
4 ounces of brie
¼ cup sliced dates
¼ cup cooked and crumbled bacon

Sauté mushrooms in butter until tender. Add sherry, Worcestershire, thyme, pepper, bacon, and dates. Remove from heat and allow to cool.

Brush 2 sheets of filo dough with butter. Layer with 2 more sheets and brush with butter. Fill with mushrooms, lengthwise, on filo dough. Lay strips of brie on top and roll into a strudel. Bake at 400 degrees for 15 minutes or until golden.

3/12/95

OW! HOT TUB! LUV,

Chris Flora

3/24 ~~26~~/95

We had a great relaxing
weekend ~ loved the
bed and the robes!
Thanks!
Petter -N- Virginia
Happy 34th Petter
Welcome Home!!!!!

Skulle ønske vi kunne være
litt lenger, for vi ble ikke
helt ferdig med badingen.
Det har vært en herlig weekend.
Petter.

Spicy Potato Strudel

1 onion, chopped
2 carrots, coarsely grated
1 zucchini, chopped
12 ounces potatoes, chopped
5 tablespoons butter
2 teaspoons mild curry paste
$\frac{1}{2}$ teaspoon dried thyme
$\frac{2}{3}$ cup water
Salt and ground black pepper
1 egg, beaten
2 tablespoons light cream
$\frac{1}{2}$ cup cheddar cheese, grated
8 sheets filo pastry
Sesame seeds

Fry the onion, carrots, zucchini, and potatoes in 2$\frac{1}{2}$ teaspoons of the butter for 5 minutes until they are soft. Add the curry paste and cook for an additional minute.

Add the thyme, water, and seasonings. Continue to cook gently, un-covered, for an additional 10 minutes.

Allow the mixture to cool and mix in the egg, cream, and cheese. Chill until ready to fill and roll.

Brush 4 filo sheets with remaining melted butter. Place 4 more sheets on top. Fill with mixture and roll. Sprinkle with sesame seeds.

Bake at 375 degrees for 25 minutes, until golden brown. Allow to stand 5 minutes before serving.

July 27, 1995

we truly enjoyed our 2nd visit to your lovely inn - and are looking forward to next time. Spring Lake is the perfect get away spot.

Johanna & Roger

8/1 - 8/4/95

(to Teddy)

Our second visit was well and what a great time we've had. Perfect as always - we even got to meet the kohlers!

Matthew + Joan

Brooklyn, NY

12/16/95

If Teddy Roosevelt would have lived in this place named for him, he would have said "foget it!" to the Spanish-American War and, in fact, preached "the doctrine of ignoble ease."

After a spell in the tub, <u>no one</u> wants to go charging up <u>any</u> hills.

(If this place were a drug, it would be illegal.)

What a great way to spend time with the one you love. With batteries recharged, it's back into the fray...

John & Sasha

P.S. John & Carol, I hope you come visit our place when we open a B&B someday.

139

June 23-25 1996

It was fun to "soak in" the
bed, and "sleep in" the
tub!
Bob & Amy

Oct. 4-5, 1996

If I were a thief, I would
take the tub and fireplace — and
the thirteen teddys, the soft glow
ceiling lights, wicker furniture, the
two standing reading lamps, chest of
drawers with mirror, the little rubber
ducky, assorted knick knacks, reading
material, the two B+B glasses and
the quaint wood flooring with all
the decorative mats! Thank you
for all these wonderful gifts and more!!
Al & Julianna
Rego Park, N.Y.

P.S. My wife actually tried to fold
up the feather bed and stuff
it in the suitcase.

Cherry Strudel

Makes 10 servings

Filling:
1¼ cups granulated sugar
½ cup firmly packed light brown sugar
1½ teaspoons cornstarch
4 cups pitted, tart, fresh or frozen, thawed cherries
⅓ cup water
2 teaspoons grated lemon or orange zest
½ teaspoon vanilla or almond extract
¼ teaspoon ground allspice
⅛ teaspoon ground cinnamon

Pastry:
8 sheets filo pastry, thawed if frozen
3 tablespoons butter, melted

Topping:
1 tablespoon confectioners' sugar

For filling:
In a medium saucepan, mix together sugar, brown sugar, and cornstarch. Stir in cherries, water, lemon zest, and vanilla. Cook over medium heat until bubbling and thickened. Reduce heat to low, add allspice and cinnamon and cook, stirring occasionally, for 15 minutes. Remove pan from heat. Cool completely.

For pastry:
Preheat oven to 400 degrees. Grease a baking sheet. Unfold sheets of filo so they lay flat. Stack 4 sheets on plastic wrap. Brush top sheet with 1 tablespoon melted butter. Keep remaining sheets covered with plastic wrap and a damp cloth to prevent them from drying out. Spread half the filling along the short side of top pastry sheet. Starting with short side and using plastic wrap as a guide, roll up pastry, jelly roll style. Fold ends under.

Place strudel, seam-side down, on prepared baking sheet. Brush with ½ teaspoon melted butter. Repeat with remaining filo, melted butter, and filling to make second strudel. Bake until golden, 15 to 20 minutes. Transfer baking sheet to a wire rack to cool for 15 minutes. Transfer strudels to a cutting board to cool completely. Sprinkle with confectioners' sugar.

Nov. 17, 1996
Just had a great bathing experience.- romantic, peaceful, relaxing and fun. We sailed the rubber duck back & forth like little kids. Tom said. "I think this is what they mean by Quality time." Now we're warm + cozy + ready to drift off. Since we can't take the tub home, I guess we'll have to come back.

Mona + Tom
5/11/97

A pleasant way to spend our 52nd anniversary (though belated 4/22) We weren't able to use the tub (too old) but enjoyed everything else
Thank you else
Lil & Harold

Some things to ponder while you stay:
1- the large diaper pin key chain
2- bright orange plunger in bathroom
3- pink flamingo's on the lawn
4 moose puppet on door hook

Donna & Ed
West Babylon, L.II/NY

Diaries from

Key to Tea Sandwiches

—*The Diaries from Velveteen Rabbit*—
*One of Carol's favorite stories growing up, she could not
resist dedicating a whole room to this whimsical fantasy.
This room, complete with its own Velveteen Rabbit,
seems to inspire trips down "memory lane" and
you'll never know what rabbit will be
peeking around the corner.*

2/15/92

To quote a line from the book itself..."the effect it had was charming."

thank you so much!
Nancy
+ Marc

May 24th

I positioned the mirrors of the walnut triple dresser to confirm my suspicions. We slipped under the fabulous Scandia down comforter and shut the light off. I kept one eye imperceptively open and with it I spied on the mirror. It was true! The velveteen rabbit and the skin horse spoke about spiritual matters. The rabbit with the long floppy white ears and the pink flowered dress leaped on the window sill and made shadow puppets with the moonlight that beamed through the window. I closed my tired eyes and tried to find my way back to Spring Lake.

Liz Lezzy

All our tea sandwiches fillings are made ahead.
Now is the time to use your "Wonder Bread" or
other thin, soft store bought bread.

Trim off the crusts and fill with desired fillings.
Cut sandwiches into 3 - 4 pieces.
Serve with a scone and some lemon cake cookies
for a "proper" tea.

April 1 1995

A beautiful early-spring
weekend. We shared it with
our closest family members
who are also our dearest
friends. We laughed, played
games, enjoyed dinner
at the Old Mill Inn, and
relaxed.

The morning starts with
a fabulous breakfast and
ends in the most comfortable
bed — the hours in between
are filled with the
things memories
are made of.

Phil and Marilyn

Smoked Turkey and Apple Chutney

Yield: 1 cup

2 apples, diced small
¾ cup cranberries
1 red onion, diced
1 orange, juice and peel
1 sprig thyme
1 sprig sage
1 sprig rosemary
1 teaspoon cinnamon
2 - 3 slices smoked turkey

Place all ingredients, except turkey, in saucepan and cover. Simmer for 20 to 30 minutes, until the apples are soft and the cranberries have popped. Remove the herb sprigs. Chill the mixture. Spread chutney on bread and lay 2-3 slices of smoked turkey on top.

Brie Spread

Yield: 4 cups

1½ tablespoons butter
½ red onion
Juice of one lemon
1 cup diced, cooked ham
8 ounces Brie cheese
1 tablespoon honey
1 teaspoon Dijon mustard

In a skillet, melt 1 tablespoon butter. Slice the red onion and add to the butter. Dice apples into small pieces; sprinkle with lemon and add to the onion. Sauté until the apples are soft and onion is cara-melized. While the mixture is still warm, place in a large mixing bowl with ham, brie, honey and mustard. Mix well and chill.

April 18, 1995
the eve of my 56th
birthday

How can I be this "old"
when I still feel so young? The child
in me is always filled with curiosity
which brought us to this charming
Inn.

And how appropriate to be given
this special room. Our oldest son had
his own velveteen rabbit an orange & white
"Petey" that he slept with every nite.

Last year I was cleaning the attic and
found "Petey", quite worn with one eye
missing. I couldn't bear to throw him
away — too many memories & hugs were
invested in him by Eric.

So for Eric's 35th birthday, I
attached a bow tie made of money around
Petey's neck & wrapped him in a
decorated box and presented this gift
to Eric at a family birthday dinner. I
told him he would never guess its
contents!

Well when he opened it and found
his Petey, tears rolled down his cheeks.
I might add there wasn't a dry eye
at the table.

148

Petey now resides with his old pal
in a small rocking chair in the living
room. Sherrie, his wife agreed to keep him.
  Eric is a fine father with two
children ~ Petey keeps his one good eye
on all of them.
  The gloomy day may   4/19
be outside, but lots of warmth and joy
inside provided by John. Carol made
our short stay a real treasure. Breakfast
was a feast.
  I'm sure we'll be back
              Barbara & Paul

                    July 13, 1995

Last night there was a full
moon. It was the last final
touch in these last two days
that allowed me to "let it all
go". Sea Crest by the Sea is
so adorable. I can't wait to
go home and tell my friends
so that they too can come and
enjoy the physical and emotional
respite
              Ernie & Margarita

149

OH, TO BE A KID AGAIN! TO BE WRAPPED IN THE EMBRACE OF A NURTURING BED WITH SOME-BUNNY YOU LOVE, THE WARM GLOW OF THE FIREPLACE CASTING SOFT SHADOWS, THE ~~ADORING~~ INNOCENT GAZE OF "MR. HOPS"... TO WAKE TO THE AROMA OF A COUNTRY BREAKFAST, FRESH SQUEEZED ORANGE JUICE, FLUFFY BLUEBERRY PANCAKES, FRESH BREWED COFFEE. THANK YOU MOM AND DAD KIRBY FOR ALLOWING US TO REGRESS AND FOR MAKING US FEEL LIKE PART OF THE FAMILY. WE SHALL RETURN, TO BE YOUNG AGAIN!

Scott + MARY

August 2-4 1996

What a perfect place to rekindle the romance! From relaxing on the veranda with a glass of wine, strolling on the beach, savoring the extravagant breakfasts, and adjusting the mirrors on the vanity just so(!) this was all in all the perfect getaway. We hate to leave. We will be sure to come back

Jaura + Steve

150

Roasted Pepper and Cucumber Sandwiches

1 cucumber, sliced thin
1 red bell pepper
Lemon juice
Salt and pepper
Olive oil

Preheat oven to 450 degrees. Place the cucumber slices in a colander and toss with the salt. Let sit for 30 minutes, then pat dry. Sprinkle cucumbers with lemon juice.

Meanwhile, slice pepper in half. Remove the stems and seeds. Brush with olive oil on all sides. Place peppers, skin side up, in oven for 20 minutes (they will smoke, but this is where the flavor comes from); watch them carefully. The skin will begin to blacken and bubble. Remove from oven at this point. Let peppers cool. Using your fingers, peel the skin off and discard. Slice the peppers into thin strips. Layer with the cucumbers and peppers to make sandwiches and sprinkle with black pepper.

BLT Sandwiches

Yield: 1 cup

¼ pound bacon
2 plum tomatoes
½ cup mayonnaise
Several leaves of lettuce

Cook the bacon until crisp. Drain the fat and cool. Once cool, crumble the bacon. Dice tomatoes and stir into mayonnaise along with the bacon. Spread mixture on bread and top with lettuce.

November 24, 1996

Yes! These have been the best three days! We've only been together for a month now but I feel like I know her better than I know myself. We were able to explore each other's inner selves physically, emotionally, & spiritually.

We felt like we were thousands of miles away in a fantasy of our own — just like the the Velveteen Rabbit, we became real and came to life! Thanks for a lovely weekend!!

Love,
Marie & Angela

P.S. The Bed squeaks!

Southern Chicken Salad

Yield: 2 cups

1 cup cooked, diced chicken breast
1 peach, peeled and diced
½ cup chopped pecans
¾ cup mayonnaise
Salt and pepper to taste

Combine diced chicken, peach, pecans, and mayonnaise; add seasonings. Chill until ready to serve.

Curried Chicken Salad

1 cup cooked, diced chicken breast
½ cup crushed (canned) pineapple, drain well
¾ cup mayonnaise
1 teaspoon mild curry
¼ teaspoon cardamom
Salt and pepper
1 tablespoon fresh or ½ teaspoon dry thyme

Combine diced chicken, pineapple, mayonnaise, curry, cardamom, salt and pepper, and thyme. Chill until ready to serve.

Dec. 15 - 96

This is our 5th time comming to the Sea Crest. We love it here so much. We come for the Christmas season each year, because we feel so great here at a time when life is so hectic. I know we will be back again next year to be together in a way that we just can't be at home. Well Merry Christmas

Cathy + Mike

P.S. The Bed Squeaks, often!

April 18 - 20

Thank you for a wonderful weekend. The food was terrific, the room charming + the atmosphere was perfect, for our "first anniversary"

Tom + Jennifer

P.S. The Bed SQUEAKS - A Lot!

Diaries from

Key to Sauces

—The Diaries of Mardi Gras—
Complete with feather masks, black satin gloves, and a real
feather boa, the Mardi Gras room has a festive air.
Moreover, this room is situated in the "turret" of the house,
lending cheerful sunshine the opportunity to bathe the
brightly colored room. Well, we know that a party
atmosphere brings out the wild side in people,
but we never even knew how wild!

AUGUST 24, 1991
- A LONG DRIVE FROM NEW YORK CITY, BUT ME +
"WHAT'S HER NAME" HAD QUITE A KINKY NIGHT
- THANKS FOR THE LATE NITE ANTISEPTIC!
    - MARV ALBERT
    NBC SPORTS

Your Mardi Gras room gave
us a night of festive
romance; warm sunrises
and colorful conversation
over imported cafe de jur
and eclectic diddy's to
nosh on.

Refreshed and rejuveniated
we leave in a better frame
of mind, knowing we'll
be back
        Anette & Mike
        of Spring Lake and
        Pittstown
        11/29/92

Fresh Strawberry or Blueberry Syrup

Yield: 2 cups

1 pint strawberries, hulled and halved or
16 ounces frozen strawberries (see note)
1 cup sugar
¾ cup light corn syrup

Mash strawberries slightly. Place strawberries in saucepan and cook until boiling.

Line a strainer with cheese cloth and place over bowl. Pour strawberries into strainer and mash to extract juice; discard pulp.

Put juice back into saucepan and add sugar and corn syrup. Cook until boiling, 10 to 15 minutes. Skim foam from top. Store in refrigerator. This recipe can be made using any berry.

Note: If using frozen strawberries, cook an additional 15 minutes.

April 3, 1994

OUR ROMANCE BLOSSOMS THE SPRING TIME. THE SURROUNDING WARMTH AND COMFORT WAS A REFRESHING BREAK FROM THE CITY. HAPPY EASTER.

Thanks
DON + THERESA

May 13-15

I don't know why everyone raves about the feathered boa when black satin gloves can be sooo... interesting

Extremely relaxing, great hospitality, a perfect retreat from the maddening world.

May 28, 1994
We had a delightful night in The Mardi gras room and especially enjoyed the "accessories"! Thank you for a relaxing and comfortable stay-
Sincerely,
Karen and Stan

CHICAGO, IL

White Sauce

Basic Recipe

Yield: 1 cup

2 tablespoons butter
1½ - 2 tablespoons flour
1 cup milk or half-and-half

Melt butter in saucepan; stir in flour. Stir in milk and simmer until thick and smooth.

Glazes

1 - 2 tablespoons apricot brandy
1 - 2 tablespoons walnut extract
1 - 2 tablespoons maple syrup
1 -2 tablespoons rum
1 - 2 tablespoons Grand Marnier
1 - 2 tablespoons fresh lemon juice or lemon extract

¾ stick of butter
1½ cups confectioners' sugar

Melt butter in saucepan and stir in your choice of a flavor. Using a mixer, add sugar and blend until smooth. Drizzle over cakes, desserts, muffins, ice cream, etc.

Great Place! June 9, 1995
Great b-day!

Bill + Liz
Upper Montclair NJ

June 18, 1995

What a great way to spend
our 1st Anniversary! It
was relaxing & romantic.
Thanks
Charles & Gayle

We came
We saw!
We Come? Taz '95
Rusty & July

Florentine Sauce

Yield: 2 cups

1 cup white sauce (see recipe on page 159)
Dash hot pepper sauce
2 drops Worcestershire sauce
1 cup chopped spinach
Nutmeg to taste
Parsley

Prepare white sauce. Blend in hot pepper sauce, Worcestershire, spinach, nutmeg and parsley. This sauce can be thinned with white wine.

Alfredo or Primavera Sauce

1 cup white sauce (see recipe on page 159)
$\frac{1}{4}$ cup finely chopped onion or shallot
1 egg yolk, beaten with 2 tablespoons cream
$\frac{1}{4}$ cup Parmesan cheese or goat cheese

Prepare white sauce. Blend in onion and egg yolk which has been beaten with cream; add slowly to white sauce with a whisk. Add Parmesan or goat cheese and blend.

Cheddar Cheese Sauce

2 cups white sauce (see recipe on page 159)
2 cups cheddar cheese
1 teaspoon dry mustard
$\frac{1}{4}$ teaspoon paprika

Prepare white sauce. Blend in cheese, mustard, and paprika.

August 26, 1994

Having met in Venice, Italy around the Carnevale time of year, it was really fitting to stay in the turret 'Mardi Gras'. It apparently <u>rocks</u> with activity, according to the entries from former guests especially the couple who enjoyed the "accessories" very much! WHOA! That's not our style, but hearing the aria 'Nessun Dorma' and it's heroic final line 'vincerò' during a sunset, passionate moment <u>is</u>. Bless the local residents who were blasting their stereo for the neighborhood to hear! "Thank you very much" "my dears!"

C+B, NYC

TO BE IN A B&O BEDYARD IN SUNRISE & SUNSET LIGHT WITH OUR LOVE IS A RARE PLEASURE...

August 25, 1997

There once was a woman
  named Jill
Who took me to the Sea Crest
  for a thrill.
She put on a boa
And all night it was whoa!
And she even took care of the bill.

Thank you Jill I LOVE You...

Ray (Lake Mohawk, NJ)

September 3, 1997

Our third B&B and of course
we were tempted to compare it
to our last. 1) the room is smaller
2) you must hold the toilet handle
3) smaller bathroom w/ too
powerful a shower 4) keep the
fan switch on to avoid the knocking
Sound....

Vicki and Reginald

Sept. 20, 1997

Beautifully decorated, spotlessly clean, painstakingly detailed.
Nice touches: chocolates at night, hair dryer & robes.

Tips on Surviving the Bathroom:
1.) Turn the fan on to eliminate the "knocking" sound;
2.) Don't drop the soap in the shower & don't shave your legs;
3.) Hope that your shampoo soap cleans most of your body because you can't bend over to wash your feet;
4.) Remember this is your own private bathroom and it's not in the hallway!
    Thanks for a great stay!

Carole & Allen
Lincoln Park, NJ

Salsa

1 large onion, diced
2 green peppers, diced
1 red pepper, diced
6 fresh tomatoes, diced
1 cup chopped, packed cilantro
6 limes, juiced
⅓ cup tequila
2 cups corn
1 can black beans
1 can white beans
1 6-pound can tomatoes
4-6 jalapeños

Combine diced onions, peppers, tomatoes and chopped cilantro. Add lime juice, tequila, corn, beans, canned tomatoes, and jalapeños. Marinate overnight to blend flavors.

This recipe makes a lot of salsa, but can be halved or quartered.

September 28 1997

Spring Lake is gorgeous.
Thanks for the bikes, Sandy.
Mardi Gras bathroom is
ridiculously small...
Hey fix that toilet, already!
I've seen journal entries
from 1993 in this book who
note the same difficulty!
Breakfasts were delicious
great weekend.
P.S. Lose the dog at
breakfast time. I sneezed
like a maniac and will
probably remember that in
future. — XOXO. —

PS HAPPY BIRTHDAY TO MY BABY

WHAT'S THE BOA'S FOR?

Banana's Foster

Usually this dish is flamed to burn the alcohol out. Simmering will release most of the alcohol from the rum, but if you would rather—use 1 teaspoon rum extract and ˘ cup apple juice in place of rum.

Serves 8

4 tablespoons butter
¼ cup brown sugar
¼ cup maple syrup or 2 tablespoons dark molasses
¼ cup rum
1 teaspoons cinnamon
4 bananas, sliced

Melt butter in a wide skillet. Add brown sugar and stir to dissolve. Add syrup, rum, and cinnamon, stirring constantly for 10 to 15 minutes. Add bananas; stir to coat and heat 2 to 3 minutes. Serve with whipped cream or vanilla cream over ice cream or on top of pancakes.

Chocolate Sauce

1 cup heavy cream
2 tablespoons cocoa powder
1 teaspoon vanilla
1 tablespoon creme de cacao
4 ounces semi-sweet chocolate

Heat cream on the stove on in the microwave on medium heat until hot, but not boiling. Sift cocoa into cream and add vanilla and creme de cacao. Pour over the chocolate and let stand to melt. Mix well.

White Chocolate Sauce

1 cup heavy cream
1 tablespoon powdered sugar
1 teaspoon vanilla
4 ounces white chocolate

Heat cream on the stove or in the microwave on medium heat until hot, but not boiling. Sift in powdered sugar; add vanilla. Pour over white chocolate and let stand to melt. Mix well.

Brandy Jam Sauce

½ cup jam (we use peach)
¼ cup water
2 tablespoons lemon juice
¼ cup brandy

Combine the jam and water in small saucepan. Bring to a boil over medium heat, stirring to reduce slightly, about 1 minute. Remove from heat; add lemon juice and brandy. Serve over french toast, pancakes or cake.

Vanilla Cream

2 teaspoons vanilla extract
½ cup sugar
¼ cup cream cheese, at room temperature
¼ cup cream
¼ cup sour cream
6 tablespoons Marsala wine

Combine vanilla, sugar, cream cheese, cream, sour cream, and wine. Mix until smooth.

168

Diaries from

Key to Cookies

—The Diaries of Papillon—
A cocoon of butterflies, like butterflies, many of our guest
come to this warm room to grow. Once you enter,
this room seems to wrap around you, enclosing you
in a safe hide away, quiet and peaceful.

Aug 28, 1994.

As you read through this book you will find many things said about this room — well at long last the truth be told!

It is said this room is cozy and intimate. This is clearly a euphemism for claustrophobic.

It is said this room is lovely — its downright dangerous — This becomes painfully clear after you sustain a skull fracture from hitting the overhead beam (unless of course you're a Munchkin)

It is said that the sunrise is beautiful — yes only for those fools who failed to close the shades before going to bed and were awakened at an ungodly hour

It is said there is a beautiful view of the ocean — Quite frankly unless you're a giraffe and can crane your head (running the risk again of hitting your head on a beam) all you'll see is "lovely" house next door.

It is said the bed is the most

comfortable people have ever slept in.
Now let's get real. The bed has a valley
in the center and you keep falling into
it about every five minutes. — I'd call
my chiropractor in the morning, but of course
there's no phone in the room. — And all
those pillows on the bed — it takes 1/2 hour
just to unload them — and as y'all see
there's no place to put them! (The doll on
the bed is cute, however.)

  Now most people don't talk about the
The plumbing — but it is important. The
sink is very small + poorly illuminated — better
to skip shaving (you're on vacation anyway).
Of course, it's not near the toilet so that's a pain
when you want to wash your hands. You can't
even put a towel near it.

  The toilet tank fills slowly — consider this
when 2 of you are leaving and trying to rush
off somewhere.

  There's also no place to hang anything wet
without dripping the floors (which are, in fact, "lovely"
(and therefore fragrances) in the closet. ⟶

You → should've stayed in NYC

BULLSHIT - EVERYTHING THIS GUY (SAYS IS TRUE:
LET'S BE REALISTIC - WAKE UP & SMELL THE COFFEE!!!
And one last thing — be sure to block
the door sill with a towel n the hall light
will keep you up all night long.

All in all, though we had fun.
+ The weather was "great" + The beach "nice"
+ So were John, Carol, cat + dog + yes
the breakfast's were very lovely. The best
thing, of course, was This little book
Next time stay at a Ritz Carlton — This
is a Bed and Breakfast! Peter + Rosanne
(from where else — but New York, N.Y.)

Sept. 16-18

My girlfriend, who I hope to make my
wife, lives in Los Angeles. I recently moved
From L.A. to Blue Bell, PA for career reasons,
and have missed her every day for the past
two months we've been apart. I can't think
of better place for us to be reunited than
here in this romantic, albeit small, room
of butterflies. These past days have been
great and we both leave with many warm
memories (and a couple bruises on my scalp) —

Christian & Christina

172

Macaroons

These cookies are so easy and so delicious they are the perfect snack for a Sunday afternoon when you are working hard on the computer.

Yield: 3-4 dozen

14 ounce can sweetened condensed milk
12 ounces sweetened coconut
1 cup white chocolate chips

Combine condensed milk, coconut, and white chocolate chips. Drop by tablespoonfuls onto a well greased cookie sheet. Bake at 300 degrees for 12 minutes. Dip in chocolate, if desired.

November 14-15, '94

I grew up next to the ocean that the sun sets into, not the ocean from which it rises. But this was the right metaphor for starting this next part of my life.

I came here mourning a great loss. My first morning here I put on my black mourner's dress and prayed by the edge of the ocean. Then I scattered the ashes and said goodbye.

I am leaving my "cocoon of sadness" now. However did you choose this room of butterflies for me? It is time for me to fly.

Louise

From Victoria - Vancouver - Los Angeles - and Philadelphia

Brownie Mounds

A very special chocolate treat. You can't eat just one! They are best with a glass of cold milk. Thanks to Charlie for sharing this recipe.

6 squares unsweetened chocolate
⅔ cup butter
1½ cups sugar
⅔ cup corn syrup
2 eggs
2 teaspoons vanilla
3½ cups flour
1 teaspoon baking powder
½ teaspoon salt
Chopped walnuts (optional)

Melt chocolate. Cream butter. Mix butter, sugar, corn syrup, eggs, vanilla, and melted chocolate. Stir in flour, baking powder, and salt. Add chopped walnuts (optional).

Drop by rounded tablespoonfuls onto ungreased baking pan. Bake 10 to 12 minutes at 350 degrees.

Lemon Cake Cookies
Yield: 36 cookies

Cookies:
2½ cups plus 1 tablespoon cake flour or 2 cups plus 3 tablespoons all-purpose flour
¾ teaspoon baking powder
¾ teaspoon baking soda
½ teaspoon salt
9 tablespoons (1 stick plus 1 tablespoon) butter, at room temperature
1 cup plus 2 tablespoons sugar
1 tablespoon grated lemon zest
2 large egg yolks, at room temperature
1 whole large egg, at room temperature
1¼ cups sour cream, at room temperature

Glaze:
6 tablespoons (¾ stick) unsalted butter
1½ cups confectioners' sugar
3 tablespoons fresh lemon juice

Preheat oven to 375 degrees. Line several cookie sheets with parchment paper or lightly grease them with butter or vegetable oil. Sift the flour, baking powder, baking soda, and salt together into a small bowl and set aside.

Using an electric mixer on medium speed, cream the butter, sugar, and lemon zest in medium bowl until light and fluffy, about 2 minutes. Scrape the bowl.

Add the egg yolks and mix on medium speed until blended, about 10 seconds. Scrape the bowl, then add the whole egg and mix until blended, 10 seconds more. Add the sour cream and mix on medium-low speed until blended, about 8 seconds.

Fold in the dry ingredients by hand, then turn the mixer on low speed for 5 seconds. Scrape the bowl with the rubber spatula and mix on low until the batter is smooth and velvety, 10 seconds. Give the batter a stir or two with the spatula.

Drop the batter by large rounded tablespoonfuls about 2 inches apart onto the prepared cookie sheets.

Bake until the cookies puff up, are firm to the touch, and just begin to turn golden, about 12 minutes. Remove the cookies from the sheets with a spatula and place them on a cooling rack. Allow them to cool completely.

Meanwhile, prepare the glaze: Melt the butter in a small pan over low heat. Place the sugar in a medium-size bowl. Add the butter and lemon juice to the sugar and beat vigorously with a whisk until the mixture is smooth and creamy.

Once the cookies have cooled, dip the entire rounded top of each into the glaze. Place the cookies on the cookie sheets and allow them to sit until the glaze hardens, several hours.

Old-fashioned Molasses Chews

Crispy, chewy, sweet and spicy. These are John's favorite.

Yield: 2° dozen

¾ *cup salad oil*
¼ *cup dark molasses*
1¼ *cups sugar*
2 eggs
2¾ *cups all-purpose flour*
1½ *teaspoons baking soda*
1 teaspoon ground cinnamon
1 teaspoon ground ginger
¼ *teaspoon ground cloves*

In a large bowl, stir together oil, molasses, and 1 cup of the sugar. Add eggs and beat until smooth. In another bowl, stir together flour, baking soda, cinnamon, ginger, and cloves; gradually add to molasses mixture, beating until well combined. Cover tightly with plastic wrap and refrigerate for at least 1 hour or until next day.

Place remaining ¼ cup sugar in a small bowl. Roll dough into 1½-inch balls, then roll in sugar to coat. Place 3 inches apart on greased baking sheets. Bake at 350 degrees for 10 to 12 minutes or until lightly browned. Transfer to racks and let cool completely. Store in airtight container.

August 12

We had a great weekend get-
a-way here at the Sea Crest.
I for one like the odd geometric!
you find in many top-floor
rooms at Victorian Inns. The
air conditioning is a real nice
touch – some seaside inns assure
you that a ceiling fan and the
sea breeze is all you need – that's
not so true. John and the staff
were very gracious and extremely
helpful. The room was somewhat
pricey but I think we paid for!
the season. The only problematic
feature of this Papillon room lies
in the haunting little dimple-
faced doll that, regardless of
where we stashed it, kept appear-
ing over and over on our freshly
made bed. It was eerie.

Thanks for everything!
Cheryl & John

178

Jumbo Crunchy Chocolate Chip Cookies

The first time John and I visited the 1811 House, I ate at least a dozen of these cookies. Oops! We are happy they shared their recipe–it saves a lot of traveling to enjoy them!

3½ cups all-purpose flour
3 teaspoons baking soda
1 teaspoon salt
1 cup butter
½ cup margarine
1 cup brown sugar, packed
1 cup granulated sugar
1 egg
2 teaspoons vanilla
1 cup vegetable oil
1½ cups corn flakes
1½ cups oatmeal
12 ounces chocolate chips

Mix flour, baking soda, and salt together. Cream butter, margarine, and sugars. Beat in egg and vanilla. Stir in flour mixture, alternately, with oil. Stir in corn flakes, oatmeal, and chocolate chips. Chill dough for an hour before baking.

Drop by heaping tablespoons onto ungreased cookie sheet 3 inches apart. Bake at 350 degrees for 12 minutes or until golden.

Dream Bars

1½ cups flour
2 cups packed brown sugar
½ cup butter or margarine
3 eggs
1 teaspoon baking powder
1 teaspoon vanilla
¼ teaspoon salt
1½ cups coconut

Combine flour, ½ cup brown sugar, and butter until particles are fine; use low speed of mixer. Press into bottom of ungreased 13 x 9-inch pan. Bake at 350 degrees for 15 minutes. Beat 1½ cups brown sugar with eggs just until blended. Mix in baking powder, vanilla, salt, and coconut. Spread over partially baked crust. Bake 20 to 25 minutes, or until golden brown. When cold, cut with a sharp knife.

Reese's® Peanut Butter Bars

Yield: 36 bars

½ cup (1 stick) butter or margarine
¾ cup Reese's® Creamy Peanut Butter
1¾ cups sugar
1½ teaspoons vanilla extract
4 eggs, slightly beaten
1½ cups all-purpose flour
½ teaspoon baking powder
¼ teaspoon salt
2 cups semi-sweet chocolate chips or milk chocolate chips

Heat oven to 350 degrees. Grease a 13 x 9 x 2-inch baking pan. Melt butter and add peanut butter; stir until melted. Stir in sugar and vanilla. Add eggs and stir until well blended. Add flour, baking powder, and salt; stir until blended. Stir in chocolate chips. Spread batter into prepared pan. Bake 35 minutes or until top is golden brown and edges are firm. Cool completely in pan or wire rack. Cut into bars.

Diaries from

Key to Cakes

Land Ho! Time to set of on a voyage of relaxation.
A voyage that will take you to a new and wonderful place,
where work does not exist. Many of those
who stay in this room find themselves reflecting on
the journeys of life, both literal and figurative.
Set your compass and hoist the sail,
it's time for a nautical adventure.
P.S. Some say the Captain still resides here.

8~11~91

We had a great weekend aboard the Yankee Clipper. The sun was shining and the beach was perfect.

This was our first, but not last trip w/ my husband's parents who are staying in "Pussy Willow". And believe it or not, going away w/ your in-laws is not as bad as you think! We'll be back next year!

Stacey and Henry

Sept. 1992

Hey! There's no closet in this marvellous Y. Clipper! John + Carol wouldn't sleep in this room — ever!

Unhappy guests? too bad!

Overnight Coffee Cake

Now you can have freshly baked coffee cake without the early morning hassles of mixing.

Serves 12

¾ cup butter, softened
1 cup sugar
2 eggs
1 cup sour cream
2 cups flour
1 teaspoon baking powder
1 teaspoon baking soda
1 teaspoon nutmeg
½ teaspoon salt
Fruit, fresh or canned (optional)

Topping:
¾ cup packed brown sugar
½ cup pecans, chopped
1 teaspoon ground cinnamon

Cream butter in bowl. Add sugar and beat at medium speed until light and fluffy. Add eggs, one at a time, beating after each addition. Add sour cream and mix well.

Combine flour, baking powder, baking soda, nutmeg, and salt. Add to wet ingredients. Pour into greased and floured 13 x 9 x 2-inch pan.

Combine topping ingredients. Can add fruit on top of batter or under topping (optional). Sprinkle topping over batter. Cover and chill at least 8 hours. Uncover and make at 350 degrees for 35 to 45 minutes.

We did
All this in one
weekend!
6/5 - 6/7

"We are now in "ship shape"
having spent two beautiful days
at your lovely home. The Yankee
Clipper was "smooth sailing"
from the moment we two
weary seafarers arrived and
we loved being lulled to sleep
by the sea air, breeze and
our soft blue surroundings.
Thank you for your warm and
gracious Hospitality,
Lyalitta and Eric

8/16/92
RAIN, RAIN GO AWAY!!!
SEA AIR/ACID RAIN!
LOVELY HOME LOVELY HOSPITALITY
ARE YOU SURE YOU DON'T HAVE
CONTROL OVER THE WEATHER?
(WISH YOU DID)
PERHAPS NEXT YEAR...

BERT J DWIGHT

Linda's Any Fruit Cobbler

*This recipe is Sea Crest's most loved and versatile fruit cobbler.
It was given to us by our good friend and fellow innkeeper
Linda Fessler at the Hollycroft Inn. We vary the fruit according to the
season and what's on hand, sometimes mixing two or three
different fresh, frozen or canned fruits or berries for
a limitless variety of delicious combinations.*

Fruit of your choice
1 cup flour
¾ cup sugar
2 teaspoons cinnamon
2 eggs
1½ sticks of butter, melted

Preheat oven to 350 degrees. Butter a 9 or 10-inch pie plate or shallow casserole.

Generously fill pie plate or casserole approxiamately three-fourths full of your choice of fruit (drained if canned), cut in spoon size chunks or slices. Leave at least 1 inch from top of pan for topping.

Mix together flour, sugar, and cinnamon. Stir in eggs one at a time. Add melted butter. Stir the mixture until smooth.   Pour over fruit and bake 45 minutes to 1 hour, until top is golden brown.

July 27, 1993

Well, all my friends said I shouldn't go on vacation alone, but they were wrong! Three glorious days of puttering around, then coming back to this cozy room with its comfy bed and ocean views - now that's a vacation...

Coming from one hotelier to another, I must say that John and Carol are the perfect hosts, and they make the best breakfasts in town.

Kudos to Daisy, Princess and Sneakers, as well -

I'll be back!
Kathy

P.S. In what room do the "French feather bed eggs" sleep on the night before?

z z z z z   z z z z z ...

White Chocolate Cheese Cake

*Our signature cheese cake. Often served at breakfast, a decadent way to
start the day and guaranteed to put smiles on the faces of all who indulge.*

1 cup sugar
2 pounds cream cheese, at room temperature
1 teaspoon vanilla
4 eggs
8 ounces white chocolate, melted

Cream sugar and cream cheese together. Add vanilla. Beat eggs in one at
a time. Blend in chocolate.

Bake in spring form pan in water bath at 450 degrees for 20 minutes. Reduce heat to 250 degrees and continue to bake for 1 hour or until firm.
Cool thoroughly, overnight, before moving from pan. Serve with pureed
raspberries, sweetened to taste with honey or sugar.

Tart Crust

*This is the perfect basic tart crust. It takes 10 minutes to make and
it is impossible to ruin. Any fruit, canned or fresh, can be used for filling.*

9-inch tart pan
1¼ cups all-purpose flour
1 tablespoon sugar
¼ teaspoon salt
½ cup cold butter
2 tablespoons cold water

Place flour, sugar, and salt into a food processor. Process for a few seconds. Cut butter into chunks and place in food processor with mixture and
process again until crumbly. Add water, 1 tablespoon at a time, until the
dough comes together. Press into tart pan; prick the dough with tines of a
fork. Bake at 425 degrees for 8 minutes or until golden brown. Fill with
desired fruit.

JUNE 30, 1997

We enjoyed our 2nd visit here. For starters in the Room I tried the hat first, I Thought "What a small head you have." Looking carefully, it was not your hat. I checked out All the documents. I AM very impresed. Some time ago "W.W II" I sailed on the Maurentia. I got into the Book "The great Liners" very little About the Maur.. We (15,000) members of The Air Corp. Boarded the ship in Norfolk. 1st stop Rio-Des. Next stop DURBANSA. Had a problem subs chased us & we went South & it was cold From there North To the Suez Canal Picked up German PRisonas & AUSIES went to Colombo (Sri Lacka) we changed Ships Maur. went t Aus We Sailed to Bombay

P.S
18 Months Later came Home on A USA Ship VIA Aus. N.Z. New Heb. Ted
& into San Pedro Calif.

Chocolate-Orange Tart with Almond Crust

Yield: 8 servings

Crust:
2 cups whole almonds, toasted
6 tablespoons packed golden brown sugar
¼ cup (½ stick) unsalted butter, melted

Filling:
½ cup plus 2 tablespoons whipping cream
6 ounces semi-sweet chocolate, chopped
2 tablespoons Grand Marnier or other orange liqueur or brandy

⅓ cup orange marmalade
1 ounce white chocolate

For crust:
Preheat oven to 325 degrees. Finely grind almonds and sugar in food processor. Add butter and process until moist clumps form. Press mixture onto bottom and sides of 9-inch tart pan with removable bottom. Bake crust until golden brown and firm to touch, about 25 minutes. Cool on rack.

For filling:
Bring cream to simmer in small saucepan. Remove from heat; add semi-sweet chocolate and whisk until smooth. Whisk in Grand Marnier. Cool until filling begins to thicken but is still pourable, about 30 minutes.

Spread marmalade over bottom of crust. Pour chocolate filling over. Refrigerate tart until filling begins to firm but is not quite set, about 20 minutes. Hold white chocolate above tart and scrape with vegetable peeler, allowing chocolate curls to fall onto tart. Chill until filling is firm, about 2 hours. Can be made 1 day ahead. Keep chilled.

Apricot Brandy Pound Cake

3½ cups cake flour
3 cups granulated sugar
1 cup butter, softened
½ cup sour cream
½ cup apricot brandy or apricot nectar
6 eggs
1 teaspoon orange extract
1 teaspoon lemon extract
1 teaspoon almond extract
½ teaspoon salt
¼ teaspoon baking soda
Powdered sugar
Brandy Whipped Cream

Heat oven to 325 degrees. Grease and flour 12-cup bundt cake pan, 10 x 4-inch tube pan or two 9 x 5 x 3-inch loaf pans. Beat all ingredients, except powdered sugar and Brandy Whipped Cream in large bowl on low speed 30 seconds, scraping bowl constantly. Beat on medium speed 2 minutes, scraping bowl occasionally. Pour into pan(s).

Bake 1 hour 20 minutes to 1 hour 25 minutes or until toothpick inserted in center comes out clean. Cool 20 minutes; remove from pan(s) and cool completely on wire rack. Sprinkle with powdered sugar. Top each serving with Brandy Whipped Cream and, if desired, fresh fruit.

Brandy Whipped Cream

1 cup heavy whipping cream
1 teaspoon apricot brandy or apricot nectar
¼ cup sugar
2 tablespoons sour cream

Beat whipping cream and brandy in chilled bowl on medium speed 1 minute. Add sugar and sour cream. Beat 2 to 3 minutes longer or until stiff. Refrigerate any remaining Brandy Whipped Cream.

Diaries from

Key to Candies

—The Diaries of Casablanca—
You must remember this…walking into this room
is like walking into another era.
Warm lighting and wooden door beads highlight this experience.
It is no wonder that people feel drawn into the magic of Casablanca.
Play it again, Sam.

of all the Gin joints in all the
world we had to come to this one!
"Rick! Rick!"
Not now kid!

but we really love it here, if
it wasen't for that swedish
meatball and her husband bothering
us, all the time!
"Rick!, Rick!"
Not now kid!

yes, this looks like the begining
of a beautiful freindship!
"Rick!, Rick!"
all Right whadoya want?

Its tea time!

Jimmy & Chevy
10/5/91

Butter Crunch

I have eaten pounds of this candy at the house of our friends,
Sheila and John. She was kind enough to pass on the recipe.
Now it can be enjoyed by all of us and our guests.

2 sticks butter
1 cups sugar
¾ tablespoon water
1 cup walnuts, chopped in small pieces
1 8-ounce bag chocolate chips
Crushed nuts

Melt butter, sugar, and water. Bring to a boil, stirring constantly with a wooden spoon, until the candy thermometer reaches 300 to 325 degrees, it should be caramel color. Working quickly, turn off the heat and add walnuts. Stir together and drop onto cookie sheet. Spread quickly to an even thickness. Add chocolate chips. Spread quickly over hardening candy, it will melt. Then sprinkle crushed nuts on top. Cool thoroughly and break into pieces.

Truffles

8½ ounces semi-sweet chocolate
¾ cups heavy cream
2 teaspoons unsalted butter
1 tablespoon brandy or liqueur
¾ - ⅔ cup cocoa powder (plus some for coating)

Chop chocolate in food processor. Warm cream but do not boil. Pour over chocolate; add butter, brandy and cocoa, one-fourth at a time, processing in between additions. Process again. Chill overnight. Roll into balls (this gets messy) and coat with cocoa powder. Enjoy!

September 26, 1992

My husband and I planned
to come to Spring Lake together
but it happened that I
had to come alone.

My stay was relaxing,
enjoyable and Serene and
I felt confortable.
I dreamed I had company
during the night. Could
it have been Rick?

Evelyn

Honeypots

Base:
1 cup all-purpose flour
½ cup confectioners' sugar
8 tablespoons (1 stick) unsalted butter, at room temperature, cut into 8 pieces
1 egg white for glazing

Topping:
6 tablespoons (¾ stick) unsalted butter
½ cup lightly packed light brown sugar
½ cup honey
1¼ cups chopped walnuts
¼ cup heavy whipping cream
1 teaspoon vanilla extract

Preheat oven to 350 degrees. Lightly grease an 8-inch square pan with butter.

For the base: Process the flour and confectioners' sugar in food processor for 20 seconds. Add the butter and process until the dough comes together, 20 to 30 seconds.

Pat the dough gently over the bottom of prepared pan and glaze it with the egg white by pouring the egg white on the dough and tip the pan from side to side so that the white spreads over the surface. Pour off the excess.

Bake the base on the center oven rack until golden, about 25 minutes. Place the base in the refrigerator for 15 minutes to cool completely. Keep the oven on.

Meanwhile, prepare the topping: Combine the butter, brown sugar, and honey in a medium-size saucepan. Heat, stirring the mixture with a wooden spoon, over medium-low heat until it begins to boil. Boil without stirring for 5 minutes.

While the mixture is boiling, put the nuts in a medium-size bowl; add the cream and the vanilla and stir to combine.

Add the boiled honey mixture to the nuts mixture and stir the ingredients together. Pour the topping evenly over the cooled base. Bake the bars on the center oven rack until the entire surface is bubbling, about 25 minutes.

Place the pan on a cooling rack and cool for 1 hour. Then run a sharp knife around the sides of the pan and let cool completely. Cut into bars with a cleaver or very strong knife.

July 14, 1993

Regardless of all the craziness
that awaits us back home ...
"We'll always have Sea Crest."
Thanks for scrumptious breakfasts,
delightful teas, warm hospitality
and sharing your beautiful
home.
We hope to return as soon as our
schedules allow...
"This could be the beginning
of a beautiful friendship."

Joe & Susan Reda
Long Island, N.Y.

YOU REMEMBER THIS.
A KISS IS JUST A KISS
A SIGH IS JUST A SIGH.
THE FUNDAMENTAL THINGS APPLY
AS TIME GOES BY.
AND WHEN TWO LOVERS WOO,
THEY STILL SAY I LOVE YOU,
ON THAT YOU CAN RELY,
NO MATTER WHAT THE FUTURE BRINGS
AS TIME GOES BY. — SAM

JIM + CAROLYN
10/24/93

ALLONS, LE JOUR DE GLOIRE
EST ARRIVE

Index

197

Index

Index

From the Gift Shoppe

Sea Crest Gear
From sleep shirts to sweat shirts, Sea Crest Gear has you covered. All of these high quality clothes are embroidered with the Sea Crest logo.

Sleep Shirt:—Over-large natural cotton dream. Makes him feel like Lord of the Manor, and her approachable. One size. $15.

Sea Crest Sweatshirt:—Authentic pigment, dyed garment washed. Available in denim blue. Cozy, warm, and stylish. It will be a favorite. Sizes: M, L, XL. $30.

Sea Crest Tee Shirt:— Beyond navy blue is the best way to describe the color of this shirt. Classy and classic. Sizes: M, L, XL $15.

Sea Crest Mock Turtleneck—This long sleeve shirt is perfect for everything, whether it is lounging around or under a sports coat, the crisp white dazzles. Sizes: M, L, XL. $20.

Sea Crest Coffee—A winner of the NYT best coffee in the world contest. Scandinavian blend. $12/lb. Beans only.

Sea Crest Mug—A perfect compliment to Sea Crest coffee. Each one is individually hand thrown on an old fashioned potter's wheel by a singular artist/potter in Minnesota. $14.

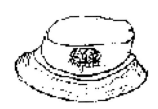

Sea Crest Vacation Hat—You won't just wait for vacation to wear this hat. A comfortable way to keep the sun out of your eyes. Available in country green. Embroidered Sea Crest logo. One size fits all. $12.50

Sea Crest Oatmeal Soap—Breakfast cereal for the soul. Sea Crest oatmeal soap. Custom made, all natural, unscented, just feels right. Three large bars. $5.

Sea Crest by the Sea, 19 Tuttle Ave., Spring Lake, NJ 07762
1-800-803-9031
www.seacrestbythesea.com
200

Buttermilk Scones

Hot and fresh from the oven and ready
for you. Decadence that was meant to
be enjoyed. $10.

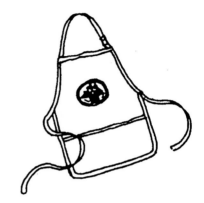

The Sea Crest Chef's Apron

When you put it on, you will beat the eggs with
more authority. Your soufflé will not fall, and
the white chocolate cheese cake will stand at
attention. This one means business. Serious
fun only. One size. Natural fiber. $15.

Sea Crest Christmas Ornament

Hand engraved scene of our Victorian cottage all
dressed up for Christmas. $5.

Sea Crest Gift Certificate

You could give her another bauble–just like last
year, or you could make a memory. A beautifully
engraved gift certificate that may be for any amount
and comes in a presentation envelope. Be a hero,
we will chill the champagne and await your
command. If it's for him, this is your chance to
renew the romance. Don't wait for a special
occasion, surprise him today.

Sea Crest by the Sea, 19 Tuttle Ave., Spring Lake, NJ 07762
1-800-803-9031
www.seacrestbythesea.com
201

I would like to order: Quantity   Amount

Dear Diary, Food for Thought/$19.95   _____   _____
Muffins and Marketing/$12.95   _____   _____
Buttermilk Scone/$10   _____   _____
Sea Crest Chef's Apron/$15   _____   _____
Sea Crest Christmas Ornament/$5.   _____   _____
Sea Crest Gift Certificate   _____   _____
Sea Crest Sweatshirt/$30   _____   _____
Sea Crest Sleep Shirt/$15   _____   _____
Sea Crest Mock Turtleneck/$20   _____   _____
Sea Crest Tee Shirt/$15   _____   _____
Sea Crest Coffee/$12/lb.   _____   _____
Sea Crest Vacation Hat/$12.50   _____   _____
Sea Crest Oatmeal Soap/$5   _____   _____
              Tax (N.J. residents only 6%)   _____
              Shipping $5.00
              Total   _____
Mail to:

Name:_____

Address:_____

City/State/Zip:_____

If gift, gift card should read:_____

_____

Enclosed is my check or please charge my account (plus tax and ship-
ping charge)
        ___Visa   ___Mastercard   ___American Express

Account #:_____

Signature:_____

Mail to: Sea Crest by the Sea
19 Tuttle Avenue, Spring Lake, New Jersey 07762
1-800-803-9031
Or visit us on the web at www.seacrestbythesea.com

Sea Crest by the Sea

*A lovingly restored 1885 Queen Anne Victorian Inn
for ladies and gentlemen on seaside holiday.
Ocean views, open fireplaces, luxurious linens, featherbeds,
buttermilk scones, and afternoon teas,
an atmosphere to soothe your weary body and soul.*

*John and Carol Kirby, Innkeepers
732-449-9031
Toll Free
1-800-803-9031
19 Tuttle Avenue
Spring Lake, New Jersey 07762*

Sea Crest Magic

We arrive on Friday terribly tight and tense.
Not talking, not touching, not together.
From the first moment, the old lady starts
to work her magic.
The light, the smells,
they all do their part.
Off to dinner in a friendly place.
Then back home to chocolates and a
bed chamber to caress us with
feathers and a fire.
Next morning, the light streams in
riding on the fragrance of
Scandinavian coffee and buttermilk scones.
Warm hugs and real talk.
Scoot down the boards young and old alike.
Idle away the day strolling the shops and
sitting on the sand staring at the sea.
By Sunday the transformation is complete.
She has done it to us again.
We have rediscovered ourselves.